THE BUILDINGS AND LANDSCAPES OF
DURHAM UNIVERSITY

THE BUILDINGS AND LANDSCAPES OF DURHAM UNIVERSITY

Martin Roberts

For
David, Mary and William
And
Those Who Watch Over

THE BUILDINGS AND LANDSCAPES OF DURHAM UNIVERSITY

© 2013 Durham University

Text © 2013 Martin Roberts

First published in 2013 by Durham University

ISBN 978 1 908990 16 7

British Library Cataloguing in Publication Data: A CIP catalogue record for this book is available from the British Library.

Designed and produced by
Third Millennium Information Limited / www.tmiltd.com

Written by Martin Roberts
Designed by Matthew Wilson
Principal photography by John Donoghue
Production by Bonnie Murray
Reprographics by Studio Fasoli, Italy
Printed by Printer Trento S.r.l., Italy

All images within the book have been taken by John Donoghue, apart from the individuals and organisations listed below who have granted permission to publish material on the following pages:

Front Cover – DU IMS 40941 • **Chapter 1: 2** – Michael Sadgrove • **Chapter 2: 9** – DULSC Add. MS 1300 no.225; **10** – DCD/N/CA/63/3; **11** – Robert Billings; **13** – DU E+B plan chest; **14** – T Sharp, Cathedral City,44; **15** – DU IMS 42942; **16** – DU IMS 46082 • **Chapter 3: 17** – DULSC UND/CK1/A2828; **18** – Martin Roberts; **19** – Jarrold/University College; **20** – DU IMS 13815; **21** – Robert Billings; **23** – DU IMS 41114; **24** – DU IMS 2217; **25** – Royston Thomas; **26** – DULSC Edis Collection Ca26; **27** – DUR UC 694, University College; **28** – DUR UC 757, University College; **29** – DU IMS 17216; **30** – DULSC UND/CK1/A1494; **32** – DULSC MS 91, f2; **35-6** – Martin Roberts; **37** – DU IMS; **39** – DU IMS 41137; **41** – Durham University; **43** – Royston Thomas; **44** – DULSC UND/CK1/A2171 • **Chapter 4: 45** – DU IMS 41100; **46** – DU IMS 40891; **52** – Bodleian Library, Gough Maps 7, 2b; **53** – DU IMS 2298; **55** – London Society of Antiquaries; **56** – Fowler; **61** – St Chad's College; **67** – DULSC OS 27.1.19; **72** – Martin Roberts; **77** – DU IMS 4092; **78** – David Darbyshire; **82** – DULSC OS27.1.23; **84** – Martin Roberts; **88** – Martin Roberts; **92** – DUR UC 693, University College; **93** – DU IMS 6536 • **Chapter 5: 94** DU IMS 38527; **95** Martin Roberts; **96** DU IMS 40952; **97** DU IMS 40941; **98** DU IMS 2257 • **Chapter 6: 100** – Gilesgate Archive, Michael Richardson; **101** – Royston Thomas; **102** – DULSC UND/CK1/BB/K1; **103** – RIBA 34935; **104** – DULSC UND/CH3/IBI (The Builder, 13-10-1944, 290); **105** – RIBA 19206 (AJ 15-6-66, 1488-3); **106** – RIBA 74668 (AJ 15-6-66, 1488-3); **107** – DU E+B plan chest; **109** – DCL Add Ms 228; **111** – DULSC UND/CK1/BB/02/7; **118** – Martin Roberts • **Chapter 7: 120** – DULSC UND/CK1/BB/L1/3; **122** – DU IMS 11804; **123** – DULSC UND/CK1/BB/E4/4; **124** – DU IMS 41066 • **Chapter 8: 130** – DU E+B; **131** – St Mary's College; **132** – DU IMS 23723; **134** – DU IMS 16016; **135** – DU IMS 2312; **136** – DU IMS 2308; **137** – DU IMS 45106; **146** – DU IMS 20834; **149** – DU IMS 41082; **151** – Oriental Museum; **152** – DU IMS 40881; **153** – DU IMS 2246; **154** – DULSC UND/F13/C6/8; **156** – DU IMS 2237; **157** – DULSC UND/CK1/A0964; **158** – DULSC UND/CK1/A0978; **159** – DULSC UND/F13/C6/5; **162** – DU IMS 6432 • **Chapter 9: 164** – Durham City Building Records 002392 (May 1949); **170** – DCRO D/X 820, 86-9; **171–2** – Martin Roberts; **173** – DULSC UND/CK1/A0770; **174** – Martin Roberts; **175** – DU IMS 7962; **176** – DU IMS 44977; **177** – DU IMS 44979; **181** – DULSC UND/CK1/BB/H5/5; **184** – DU IMS 40901 • **Chapter 10: 189** – DU IMS 42589; **190** – DU IMS 28193; **191** – DU IMS 28164; **192** – DU IMS 28159; **193** – DU IMS 42233; **194** – DU IMS 42232; **195** – DU IMS 42234.

Previous pages: The staircase (left) in Eden House, 3 South Bailey, St John's College and the window (right) in St Mary-the-Less church, South Bailey.

CONTENTS

INTRODUCTION

This book is about how Durham University has changed the face of the City of Durham over the past 180 years. The university has done great good here, and the richness of what it inherited and has conserved, and the beauty of what it built and newly landscaped, is its legacy to the city. This book is a celebration of that.

Let's start with the buildings. Durham Castle is well known to all. The faces, at least, of the peninsula colleges are well known too, as much as the fronts of South Road colleges are admired from passing cars. But what of the treasures that lie within? Bishop Cosin's Library, now wonderfully restored. The elegance of Hatfield's Birley Room and the richness of St John's Tristram Room, St Chad's diminishing gardens, Bede's chapel, St Aidan's dining hall, St Mary's great south lawn, Trevelyan's grounds and so much more. They all deserve the widest audience, so I hope that even the most well-informed of you will find some new delight here (**1**).

This book is also emphatically about Durham's landscapes, its natural topography and its man-made university landscapes of gardens and grounds. You could write a book about some of the greatest universities in this country and never mention their natural landscape once, so wonderful are their buildings, so flat are their cities. You can't in Durham. If Alexander Pope urged eighteenth-century garden designers to consult the *genius loci* in their landscapes, to find the 'spirit of the place', then the *genius* in Durham is inextricably linked to its dramatic topography, and the best buildings are those that can respond, can resonate, with that.

A note of caution. This is not a work of reference, but a personal selection of what is best and extraordinary in Durham University. I could have offered a comprehensive list of every university building, dates and architects, and you would have consulted it as often as you look at a telephone directory, and with as much pleasure.

Finally, I hope, this book conveys my love and enthusiasm for Durham. I have been privileged to know this city at close quarters for almost forty years, much of the time spent on the university estate. It never fails to fascinate.

As I have said before, elsewhere, I hope you enjoy this book, share its sense of exploration, and want to make discoveries of your own.

Opposite: *South court, St Mary's College.* (1)

6

THE LANDSCAPE OF DURHAM

THE CITY ON THE ROCK

First take a broad valley surrounded by a ring of hills. Into that bowl, comes a river, from the south, wayward at first, meandering through its flood plain, but then more incisive where it swings round to cut a deep gorge through a rocky outcrop, before turning sharply back on itself, returning north to the valley, and leaving the rock it circled almost an island.

That rocky peninsula, girded by the Wear, was a natural defensible site. It was probably occupied by Iron Age people, who would have easily cut a ditch across the northern neck to complete their protection. More certainly we know a Saxon community settled in 995 AD and around St Cuthbert's shrine, its church and monastery, a small town would have developed. Still later, the Normans built their new castle and cathedral, two of the greatest buildings in Europe, and in their shadow a medieval town grew up – a city in fact – but always a small one.

DURHAM IN ITS LANDSCAPE

The scale of those two great buildings, rising into the sky, must have astonished the native Saxon population. The cathedral especially became the focus of all eyes, the hub around which the surrounding hills circled.

That view of the castle and cathedral, set above the river gorge, became Durham's signature, unique but also paradoxical. For though both buildings dominate the skyline when seen from the river below, they disappear almost without trace beyond the bowl. To those approaching Durham, only the upper stage of the cathedral's central tower rises above the horizon. Significantly that upper stage was an afterthought, added at the end of the fifteenth century, creating one of the tallest English cathedral towers, a tower created as a direct response to Durham's setting within its landscape bowl (2).

Once built, that tower and, for a while, its western spires too, became a beacon for medieval pilgrims. When it first came into view they crossed themselves at Silent ('Signing') Bank, then dropped to lower ground and lost their beacon until just outside the city when, to great celebration, they climbed again up to Mountjoy, their journey finally at an end.

Centuries later, estate owners around Durham laid out their gardens and parks, each contriving to bring the cathedral tower, as an eyecatcher, into views from their gazebos, terraces and walks. That tradition was maintained in the twentieth century when new university colleges strove to capture and frame views of the peninsula from their buildings and courts.

This then is Durham viewed from fixed points in its wider landscape. But how is the city viewed at closer quarters, from within? Specifically, how does *moving* through Durham reveal its buildings and landscape?

MOVING THROUGH THE CITY

Let us take the natural landscape first. Durham's topography would excite the eye even without great buildings on it. The view of the peninsula rock and its encircling river would have impressed from any number of vantage points. But imagine the greater excitement of *moving* through that landscape, on foot or by boat. First the openness of the flood plain, then the confinement of the gorge, new views constantly revealed as the river swung around the rock, then out into the open valley again.

Over this complex natural landscape another complexity was laid – a medieval city. A pattern of different boroughs, interlinking streets and bridges, public and private spaces, large and small, all grew up around the great peninsular citadel of the castle and cathedral.

In all these new spaces, artificially defined by buildings, the same lessons that can be drawn from the natural environment hold good. What excites the senses in our great medieval cities is not just the intrinsic quality of the buildings, their massing, façades, decoration and sculpture, but the kinetic experience of moving between them all.

Of course, this experience is not exclusively a medieval one. Renaissance cities evoke the same aesthetic responses by the articulation of spaces – expansive, constricted, anticipatory, revelatory. Those same ingredients are also central to the eighteenth-century English Landscape movement. Designers were concerned with how the observer, *in motion,* appreciates the landscape, how distant parkland buildings may be glimpsed, then lost, teasing the viewer until the building reappears fully framed in the parkland.

UNDERSTANDING MOVEMENT THROUGH LANDSCAPES

It is one thing to enjoy the landscape, quite another to know why we are enjoying it. We like a piece of music, but unless we have a professional understanding of music, do we know why we like it? What combination of chords, what change of key, what change of tempo, is playing with our senses to evoke the right response? We need to ask why we enjoy walking through Durham – as complex a sensory experience as listening to any symphony.

An attempt to codify the urban experience was made in the 1960s and 1970s by Gordon Cullen, who invented a drawing notation for recording spatial change, and devised the term 'serial vision', for movement through a variety of different spaces. His work was celebrated in a book called *Townscape,* a word that has been taken up as defining the quality of the urban environment. By implication, Cullen's work attempted to define the moods induced by different spaces – tension in confinement, engagement with the anticipatory, joy at revelation, and serenity at expansive, composed spaces.

Those varying emotions can be appreciated in most English cities. But in those places where the natural topography is essentially flat, the pleasure in moving through them must rely wholly on the buildings to make the drama. In York, Oxford and Cambridge, what thrills is not simply the richness of great architecture, but the way those buildings frame spaces, and how those enclosures are then perforated with gates and gaps to draw the observer onward from one space to another, from market place to alley to street to collegiate quad.

Durham, on the other hand, is different. It has those same spatial complexities but laid out on a natural landscape of astonishing variety. The city is twice blessed.

TWO DURHAM WALKS

To illustrate this, let us take two journeys on the peninsula, one north to south, one east to west, ignoring, if you can, the architectural merits of the buildings. Forget their rich façades full of history and detail, just think of them as solids that enclose voids. Focus on the spaces through which you move.

For the first walk, start in the Market Place, an irregular, enclosed public space, then move south, tightening into Fleshergate and on to Saddler

*Approaching
Kingsgate Bridge
from New Elvet.* (3)

Street, still narrow, winding and rising to the foot of Owengate, all the time hemmed in by buildings and, the gradient aside, you will be quite unaware of the city's wider topography. From Owengate you rise up, still constricted, to the revelatory view of the castle and cathedral. Palace Green is yet another great space, also irregular and organic in its enclosing walls, but the space is more generous – more sky – in contrast to the Market Place where we began.

From Palace Green take an irreverent short cut across the nave of the cathedral, past another explosive view of the great church, then onwards into the cloisters – a world of private, ordered formality, four square, a place of quiet and contemplation. Finally tunnel south again under the medieval refectory, until you emerge in The College, a semi-private space, sequestered, irregular in plan – once busier, the outer court of the monastery where monks could meet the town.

This walk is as visually rewarding as any through a great historic city. But it is an almost totally urban experience, defined by buildings – walls and roofs. The natural landscape of Durham hardly plays any part.

Now let us take another journey, beginning away from the peninsula, on New Elvet, by Dunelm House (3). The river cannot easily be seen here, the path is deliberately angled, and it is only when you are squeezed between buildings, then thrown

11

out onto Kingsgate Bridge, that the Wear gorge is revealed, with the full panorama of the cathedral's Chapel of Nine Altars rising behind (**4**).

The space expands, north and south, along the river gorge, but as you reach land on the peninsula, you walk under a dark vault of trees, up onto the narrow cobbled Bow Lane, drawn on by the cathedral beckoning you ahead (**5**). Across the Bailey and up Dun Cow Lane, walking along an unbalanced street with tidy vernacular to the right and the vast cathedral cliffs to the left. Once at the top, Palace Green bursts open, the castle and the full flank of the cathedral can be seen (**6**). But don't stop, head on, across Palace Green to cut down the narrow vennel called Windy Gap, through the bedrock. At the bottom the riverbank landscape spreads out in front of you. Turn right, down Broken Walls, under the tree canopy, to the water's edge (**7**), then up the narrow steps cutting into Silver Street and out onto Framwellgate Bridge. From here the classic view of the castle, cathedral and river gorge, perfectly closed by Prebends Bridge, can be fully appreciated (**8**).

This second route delivers the same spatial variety as our first walk did, but adds a new dimension – the topography – capturing the essence of Durham as a unique melding of the built and natural landscape.

Above: *The view south from Kingsgate Bridge.* (4)

Below left: *Up Bow Lane.* (5)

Above: *Into Palace Green.* (6)

Right: *Down Broken Walls.* (7)

Far right: *Looking south from Framwellgate Bridge.* (8)

DURHAM AND ITS UNIVERSITY

The university in Durham came late to the city, in 1832. Besides its considerable social and economic value to the town, its physical impact has been dramatic. It is the purpose of this book not only to show how it has conserved the buildings it inherited, but also how in its own buildings it has responded to the city's unique topography.

Take, for example, its colleges. It might seem logical to a young nineteenth-century university, keen to aspire to the establish standards of Oxford and Cambridge, to build its colleges in imitation of those universities, quad on quad, fully enclosed

The Music School, Palace Green.

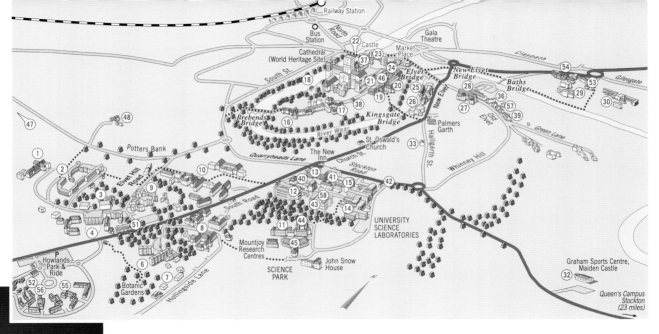

on all sides and almost monastic in their inward, exclusive, way. But look closely at Durham colleges and you will find they almost always fail to enclose, or to put it more positively, they look out, inclusively to take in the natural landscape of woods and trees, or borrow views of the great peninsular monuments to complete their missing fourth sides. Durham colleges have evolved in a manner sensitive to the signature that defines the city.

That sensitivity is not exclusively collegiate. The east-west walk described above began on Kingsgate Bridge, beside one of the university's most dramatic and groundbreaking buildings, Dunelm House. The juxtaposition of Dunelm House and Kingsgate Bridge and the journey it invites – quintessentially 'Durham' as we have seen – has been described as 'the greatest contribution modern architecture has made to the enjoyment of an English medieval city'.

The pages that follow will hopefully trace, with equal enthusiasm, the university's contribution to the development of the city for almost two centuries.

OUTLINE HISTORY

FOUNDATION

The Dean of Durham in 1831 was Dr John Banks Jenkinson. And on 31 August of that year he was a worried man, sufficiently so to share his worries in a letter to a number of his fellow canons on the Cathedral Chapter.[1] The Dean was concerned that the Reform Bill, then being debated would, when enacted, place much of the cathedral's wealth beyond the control of the Durham Chapter. He proposed a scheme to allocate a part of their income towards an enlarged system of education to be connected to the cathedral. This letter set in motion the founding of Durham University.

He was not the first to tread this path; a university in Durham had first been mooted under Henry VIII.[2] A more serious attempt was made in 1650 to establish a college in the former prebendal houses of the Dean and Chapter. Letters patent were issued, and a provost and fellows nominated, but, after an attempt to gain university status in 1658/9, it survived only until the Restoration a year later.

Under Dr Jenkinson's plan, the Durham College, as it was first to be known, was to have a Master or Principal, later Warden, and three professors – Divinity, Greek and Latin, and Mathematics and Natural Philosophy. The foundation was to be funded by 20 per cent of the net income of the Cathedral Chapter.[3]

Matters moved swiftly. One of the canons, Archdeacon Charles Thorp, was appointed Warden in December 1831, and the University of Durham Act was passed on 4 July 1832, less than a year after the Dean's letter (9).[4]

Palace Green in 1835 (Joseph Bouet). (9)

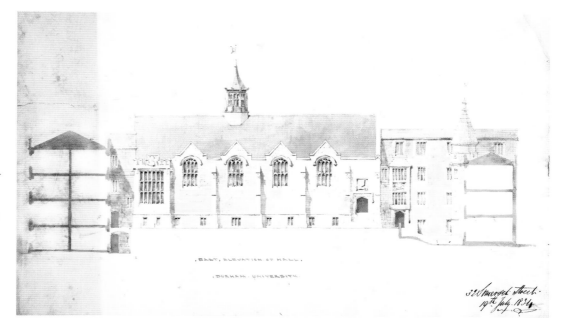

Right: *Anthony Salvin's proposed new college on Palace Green: courtyard elevation of the dining hall.* (10)

Below: *Durham Castle from Crossgate (Robert Billings 1844).* (11)

To make temporary provision for the first students, admitted in the Michaelmas Term of 1833, lodgings were secured in the Archdeacon's Inn (now Bishop Cosin's Hall) on Palace Green. This was not a permanent solution and in June 1834, Anthony Salvin, as the cathedral architect, was directed to make plans for new college buildings on the west side of Palace Green (**10**).[5]

In June 1837 a royal charter confirmed the constitution of the university; two months later, after the death of Van Mildert the previous year, the new university appropriated his old palace, Durham Castle (**11**). Salvin's Palace Green college plans were set aside and he was asked instead to restore the ruined castle keep as student rooms, a task completed in 1840.

Durham University was always intended to be a collegiate university, and for its first 14 years University College, based in the castle, was its solitary college. It was joined in 1846 by Hatfield Hall (later College), where Anthony Salvin was again called upon to design new student rooms. A third college, Cosin's Hall, based in Bishop Cosin's Hall on Palace Green, lasted only from

1851 to 1864, when it was effectively absorbed by University College.

Alongside the expansion in Durham, developments were taking place in Newcastle upon Tyne. In 1852 the Newcastle School of Medicine was founded and, together with medical schools in London and Birmingham, was formally associated with Durham University. In 1871 a School of Physical Science was established in Newcastle, fully incorporated into Durham University in 1874.

NINETEENTH-CENTURY DEVELOPMENTS

The growth in educational opportunity in Durham during this period saw the birth of institutions which were later to form part of the collegiate structure of the university. Two independent teacher training colleges were established: Bede College (for men) was founded in 1839 and St Hild's College (for women) followed in 1858, both later forming St Hild and St Bede College (**12**).

Against these growth areas, in the university itself the middle years of the century were marked by a decline in student numbers; by 1860, matters had reached a critical point. Student numbers had fallen to 51, the university's finances were in serious trouble and Durham was perceived as both being expensive and having a poor academic reputation.[6]

Warden Thorp, however, refused to change course. A Royal Commission followed, reporting back in 1862, proposing radical re-organisation. In the aftermath, Thorp was removed, while the Dean took over. The Dean's proposed changes, based on an 1865 report, were not that successful, and so, in 1870, in a further effort to expand, the university admitted students not living within a college, more often at home – the 'unattached'.

Durham University first admitted unattached male students in 1871. In 1888 they formed themselves into St Cuthbert's Society, which became the recognised designation for non-collegiate male

Above: *St Hild's College as first built in 1858.* (12)

Below: *Proposal for the enlargement of the Dawson Building, Lower Mountjoy. 1937.* (13)

students in 1947. Unattached women students were admitted in 1895, and in 1947 they became known as St Aidan's Society (later College in 1961).

The university's first women students in Durham matriculated in 1896, all from St Hild's College. In 1899 a women's hostel was set up in a house on Palace Green, which in 1919 became known as St Mary's College.

1900–39

From its foundation in 1832 the Dean and Chapter had endowed the new university with land, in Durham itself, to accommodate the university's facilities, and also further afield, to generate an income that would support the new enterprise. A further major endowment was made in 1839–40. By 1904, the university portfolio included its principal asset on the Durham peninsula as from the castle (N) to the cathedral churchyard (S), and bounded by the river on the E and W, including Palace Green, large parts of North Bailey and

Hatfield Hall. Beyond the city centre it owned the Racecourse and held rural estates to the south and west, as well as large landholdings at South Shields.[7]

1904 also saw the establishment of a new independent theological hall, St Chad's, followed in 1909 by another, St John's. Both took the style and title of independent colleges within the university in 1919.

The 1908 University of Durham Act introduced a federal system with two divisions – Durham and Newcastle – the latter known as King's College from 1937. It also moved the management of university away from the Dean and Chapter to a new body – a Senate – with a chancellor, vice-chancellor, and two pro vice-chancellors.[8]

In 1924 the university began to grow beyond the peninsula, building its first Science Laboratories (now Dawson Building) at the foot of South Road.

Little development took place in the university during the years of austerity in the late 1920s and 30s, although a significant extension was added to the Dawson Building in 1939/40 (**13**). Pressure for Newcastle Division's separation from Durham mounted, but to no avail. Expansion was talked of in Durham, and St Mary's College even drew up plans for a new building in the late 1930s, but all was put on hold in the years leading up to the beginning of World War II in 1939.

1944–60

Durham escaped the war with no bomb damage, but the city was beginning to suffer from increased vehicular traffic and its consequent decline as a retail centre. The university, secure on its peninsular site, was not immune from these problems, dependent as it was on the neck of the peninsula providing the vital access. It also had ambitions to grow, post-war, and that meant off the peninsula, but where? With the end of the hostilities in sight, increasing attention was being paid to the post-war reconstruction and redevelopment across the country. In 1944 the city fathers turned to Thomas Sharp, one of the most acclaimed of the new town

Thomas Sharp's proposed plan (1944) for three new colleges on the north bank of the Wear. (14)

planners, and a native of County Durham, to prepare his *Cathedral City – A Plan For Durham*. Amongst a great deal else, his report examined the expansion of the university, and he recommended that the new 'through road' across the neck of the peninsula provided the best artery off which to develop five new colleges, south of Claypath and Gilesgate, facing the river (**14**).

In response to Sharp's proposals, three years later the university commissioned its own plan from the architect Prof. JS Allen. Allen's plan proposed extensive demolition in the town to

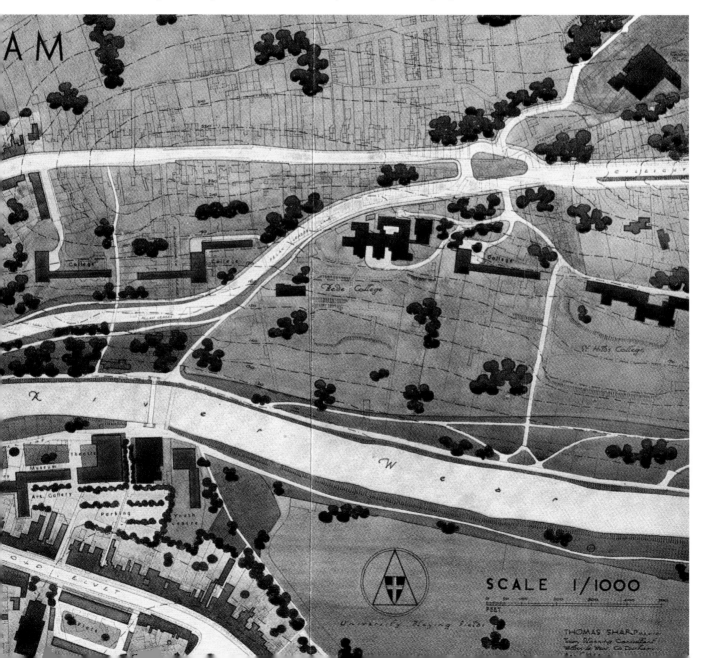

SCALE 1/1000

THOMAS SHARP

Opposite: The Institute of Hazard and Risk Research (right) and the 'West Building' (centre). (15)

accommodate new university buildings, but a combination of local protest and development opportunities in Elvet in the late 1950s and early 1960s avoided this, instead allowing a more unobtrusive assimilation on the peninsula.

At the South Road Science Laboratories site (now Lower Mountjoy) Allen proposed expansion, and land was being acquired for this purpose in 1949.[9] In 1952 his own West Building (**15**) was built there. On Allen's design team was the young (now Sir) William Whitfield, an architect whose influence on the city, and the University in particular, over the next 40 years, was to be considerable.

In the same year the independence of the Newcastle Division, now with three times more students than at Durham, was again considered and again rejected.

In the 1950s universities had to balance the political and popular demand for increased higher education provision with a prolonged period of post-war financial austerity. The pressure for expansion had begun as far back as the late 1940s when, after the end of the war, student numbers began to increase rapidly. In Durham, St Mary's College was provided with new buildings in 1952, followed, seven years later, by Grey College, Durham's first new post-war college.

1960–2012

Towards the end of the 1950s, Durham University had just over 1400 students, living in eight colleges.[10] By 1968 numbers had more than doubled to 3,000 students in 12 colleges – an expansion driven by both national and regional considerations. In 1960 the government had alerted all universities to the need to accommodate significant growth in student numbers, setting 1963 as the start of this expansion. In Durham the university responded by updating and revising J S Allen's 1947 Master Plan. In 1963 the government's Robbins report gave further impetus to university growth, and within the North East this national expansion programme led to the final break with King's College, when the University of Newcastle upon Tyne was established in its own right. The loss of Newcastle's science facilities meant that they needed to be provided in Durham alongside current building projects.

This period of rapid expansion coincided with the university's move into New Elvet, where it acquired land in the late 1950s and built in the early 60s. The move into Elvet added another centre for the university along with the peninsula and the more distant Science Laboratories (Lower Mountjoy). The peninsula and Elvet were elegantly united by Ove Arup's Kingsgate Bridge (1962–3), high above the river gorge, and alongside it Dunelm House Students' Union was constructed 1963–6, designed by the Architects Co-Partnership. The university saw this building as the first phase of a four-site development of the whole of the west side of New Elvet, providing arts facilities that could not be accommodated on the peninsula. A master plan for these sites was produced by Prof. Jack Napper incorporating Dunelm House on the southernmost site, and the new Arts Building (now Elvet Riverside 1) on the central of the three sites to the north.[11] Elvet Riverside 2 was, after some years, to occupy the southern of these sites, but the northernmost site, which would have destroyed many of the historic buildings at the junction of Elvet Bridge and New Elvet, never materialised.

When Durham County Council finally built its new County Hall at Aykley Heads in 1963, the university bought its Old Elvet properties, principally Old Shire Hall and a large number of buildings opposite, installing their administrative office into Old Shire Hall, with several Arts departments across the road.

Subsequent new building off the peninsula was concentrated to the south of the city, where the expanding university estate included not only the Science Laboratories but also the well-landscaped and wooded nineteenth-century estates of Elvet Hill, Oswald House and Hollinside.

Allen's 1947 master plan had already allocated this area for university development and a revision to the plan in 1960 proposed a total of nine new colleges there, including the existing St Mary's and Grey Colleges. In the first phase, starting in 1963, the university planned to establish three new colleges. By the early 1970s they had been built, Van Mildert (1962–5), Trevelyan (1965–7) and Collingwood (1971–4), together with a new building for the existing St Aidan's College (1962–4).

Alongside the early Science buildings at the foot of South Road (Lower Mountjoy), new buildings were commissioned, starting with a new Science Library (1963–5) by William Whitfield, followed by the opening of the Chemistry, Geology and Maths building in 1964, with the Engineering Building completed the following year. Back on the peninsula, expansion of the Arts Library on Palace Green was provided in a superb addition by George Pace (1961–6).

In 1969, having achieved their 1971 target of 3000 students the year before, the university put forward proposals for even further expansion over the next ten years.[12] The plan was given a more tangible form soon after in the University Development Plan, prepared by William Whitfield, anticipating growth up to 1980.

The conservation area in the centre of Durham had first been designated in 1968, and in 1980 it was greatly enlarged by the City Council. Such measures and the growing awareness of the cultural value of the nation's townscapes, not just its principal historic buildings, prevented any further occurrence of the major clearances seen in New Elvet in the 1960s. New large-scale university development in Durham could only be accommodated on the land it held south of the city and in 1978 William Whitfield's new Business School opened there.

In 1986, the quality of the peninsula's unique architectural heritage was recognised by the inscription by UNESCO of the castle and cathedral as a World Heritage Site.

In the 1980s and 90s when central government again drove forward an agenda of university expansion, new science buildings were constructed at Lower and Upper Mountjoy, along with additional student accommodation at most of the South Road colleges. The target could not be met solely by additions to existing colleges, and in 1994 a major new college was planned at Howlands Farm, still further out along South Road (now Ustinov and Josephine Butler Colleges).

The 1990s also saw the development of Queen's Campus, Stockton, first proposed in 1987. The first-phase buildings opened there in 1992, with a second phase commencing in 1998. The gradual development of Lower Mountjoy was brought into a more co-ordinated whole by the extensive landscaping there completed in 2012.

The closure of Ushaw College in 2011 prompted the strengthening of ties with the university to explore new joint uses of the site and extend library cooperation. Back in Lower Mountjoy, the new Palatine Centre, Law School and Library extension was opened in 2012 (16).

Palatine Centre. (16)

THE PENINSULA: PALACE GREEN

03

SETTING

If the spiritual centre of Durham lies in the stillness around St Cuthbert's shrine, its cultural heart is surely Palace Green, the great space set out eight centuries ago to bring a Bishop's palace closer to his cathedral. Out went the Saxons and in their place Bishop Van Mildert laid out a great square – only recently a green one – around which he and his successors set out the palatinate offices that symbolised their secular power in the North (17).

The approach to Palace Green, arriving in it, its sense of space and the leaving of it, has been described in the preceding chapter. In that account what was being considered was the changing sense of enclosure and exposure. In the following chapters we go behind the façades of buildings to explore them in detail, their history, their architecture and something of the people that inhabited them.

Aerial view of the peninsula. (17)

Plan of Durham Castle. (18)

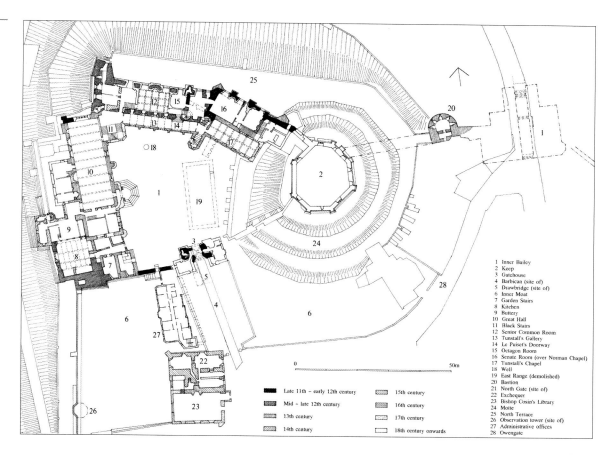

1 Inner Bailey
2 Keep
3 Gatehouse
4 Barbican (site of)
5 Drawbridge (site of)
6 Inner Moat
7 Garden Stairs
8 Kitchen
9 Buttery
10 Great Hall
11 Black Stairs
12 Senior Common Room
13 Tunstall's Gallery
14 Le Puiset's Doorway
15 Octagon Room
16 Senate Room (over Norman Chapel)
17 Tunstall's Chapel
18 Well
19 East Range (demolished)
20 Bastion
21 North Gate (site of)
22 Exchequer
23 Bishop Cosin's Library
24 Motte
25 North Terrace
26 Observation tower (site of)
27 Administrative offices
28 Owengate

Late 11th – early 12th century
Mid – late 12th century
13th century
14th century
15th century
16th century
17th century
18th century onwards

0   50m

UNIVERSITY COLLEGE (DURHAM CASTLE)

It is one of the delightful paradoxes of the university's history that, by receiving Durham Castle in 1837, it immediately acquired probably the oldest 'university' building in the country. Far more significant and incontestable was its 1986 inscription as a World Heritage Site with the cathedral. What alone could justify that status for the castle is the great rarity and quality of its medieval buildings – once the palace home of the bishops of Durham.

When William the Conqueror's army displaced the Saxons in Durham in 1069 they found a peninsula site naturally protected by the river gorge, vulnerable only at its northern neck. Almost certainly the Saxons had fortified the site before the Community of St Cuthbert brought the body of their saint onto the peninsula in 995. But the expulsion of the Saxons from the peninsula was short-lived; they counterattacked, slaughtered William's army and murdered his newly appointed Earl of Northumbria.

The Norman castle-palace (1072–1217)

William's revenge was the infamous Harrying of the North, and in Durham he refortified the peninsula by building the castle (**18**). Work began in 1072 under the new earl, Waltheof. But after his murder in 1076 the earldom was sold by the king to the Norman bishop, Walcher (1071–80). In so doing William established the future bishops of Durham as the military commanders protecting his northern border against the Scots, and also the spiritual leaders of the Durham diocese. The castle remained the principal residence of the bishops of Durham, its outer walls embracing the whole of the peninsula, including the cathedral and its priory.

Bishop Walcher faced two tasks in continuing the building work – to establish a fortress that would consolidate their hold on the region and to provide a residence fit for one of the most powerful men in the north of England. Durham Castle needed to be both castle and palace.

The early work of the bishops of Durham in the north and west ranges of the castle gives a very rare glimpse into the architectural scale and lavishness of the palaces of Norman England.

The motte was raised with a timber tower on its top, around which a stone ring wall was later added. From its heights, the castle garrison could overlook the inner bailey to the west and the main entrance to the peninsula, the North Gate, to the east.

The inner bailey was enclosed with ranges of buildings on the north, east and west sides, with the gatehouse and perhaps other buildings to the south. The north wall was a freestanding structure of c.1072 before the building now known as the chapel was constructed against it, probably in the 1080s, as part of a larger, two-storey range. This chapel is one of the most powerful expressions of early Norman architecture in the country (**19**). The internal space is divided by two rows of three columns into 12 small groin-vaulted compartments. It is built entirely of local sandstone, including its

The Norman chapel, Durham Castle. (19)

herringbone paving, an original feature. The circular columns have the most astonishing natural veining and are crowned with primitively sculpted capitals of energetic designs. The room was originally lit by three small east windows, now blocked, and two windows inserted into the earlier north wall which were later widened. The lack of windows on the more secure south side, the obvious place for good light, must indicate that a building abutted here.

The mid-twelfth-century castle is vividly described by Laurence, Prior of Durham *c.*1144–9. Of the chapel he says, 'There is also a shining chapel here supported upon six columns not too large, but quite lovely'. His account prompts the question as to whether the chapel 'supported *upon* six columns' refers not to the surviving building, but to one, now gone, that may have stood above

it. Both may have been chapels, double chapels being a feature of royal and episcopal palaces.

A great hall was established in the west range of the inner bailey in the late eleventh century. Its undercroft still exists with a broad central wall of plain arches (**20**).

To the south, against the edge of the inner moat, the lowest levels of the present kitchen and Garden Stair building are of Norman date. Further to the east was an eleventh-century gatehouse leading out across the moat with a wall rising up to the motte again. At the base of the motte on the east side of the courtyard once stood a further range of buildings.

Bishop Flambard is credited with the rebuilding of the gatehouse in the south range in the early twelfth century. Though much altered in later centuries, the surviving entrance arch with its thinly

The late eleventh-century undercroft of the great hall, Durham Castle. (20)

Bishop le Puiset's late twelfth-century doorway in the north range, Durham Castle (Robert Billings 1844). (21)

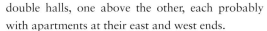

Right: *The Norman Gallery. Bishop Le Puiset's late twelfth-century north range, Durham Castle.* (22)

Below: *Interior of the great hall looking north, Durham Castle.* (23)

incised zigzag design looks very like work in the cathedral nave.

In about 1155 the west side of the town suffered a serious fire, which badly damaged the castle. The rebuilding was undertaken by Bishop Hugh of Le Puiset (1153–95), one of the greatest of Durham's 'builder-bishops'. His major work was the rebuilding of the fire-damaged north range, where he erected double halls, one above the other, each probably with apartments at their east and west ends.

The lower hall stood above an ancient sandbank, possibly a vestige of pre-Conquest or early Norman earthworks. Le Puiset gave this new hall a ceremonial entrance, reached up a flight of steps from the main courtyard. Its doorway is richly decorated and quite without parallel in the North of England (21).

Most of Le Puiset's lower hall has disappeared, but the Norman Gallery above represents his upper hall (22). The whole of the south and most of the north walls survive as a magnificent arcade of windows in alternate bays, their arches supported on columns, with raised bases forming window seats, the whole richly decorated with zigzag. The evidence of this room and its great entrance doorway suggest Le Puiset's range was of such opulence that it can have had few equals in the kingdom.

The later medieval castle (1284–1559)

For over a century after Le Pusiet's work, successive thirteenth-century bishops saw no reason to undertake major improvements. It was not until the arrival of Bishop Bek (1284–1311) that once again major building began with a new hall in the west

The courtyard of Durham Castle, with Bishop Tunstall's gallery, tower and chapel (left and centre) and the remodelled keep of 1839–40 (right). (24)

range (**23**). Built over the old undercroft, much of the present hall is Bek's work. The finely arched entrance doorway is his, as is the southernmost window on the west side of the hall.

In the second decade of the fourteenth century Durham fell prey to the annual attacks of the Scottish king, Robert the Bruce, and the principal entrance to the castle, the North Gate in Saddler Street, was refortified with a barbican (after 1313) and the addition of a large bastion tower between the gate and the castle keep.

Later in the century, in more settled times, Bishop Hatfield (1345–81) continued the aggrandisement of the castle. He lengthened Bek's great hall southwards, renewed the roof and most of the windows on the east and west sides and inserted a double window, now partially blocked, in his new south wall (**24**).

He also rebuilt the ancient Norman keep, widening the motte to accommodate it. The new keep was an irregular octagon, a shell keep, with four storeys of apartments over vaulted basements, lined against the outer walls so as to leave a central well open to the sky. It was something of an anachronism, remote from the principal ranges around the courtyard, yet a highly symbolic building, raised high above the town. Similarly, at the beginning of the fifteenth century, Bishop Langley's impressive rebuilding of the North Gate was perhaps done as much for show as for defence.

Hatfield's keep stood for over 100 years before the castle itself underwent a further major rebuilding programme during the episcopate

Bishop Fox's 1499 buttery and servery hatches, Durham Castle. (25)

of Bishop Fox (1494–1501). Much of his work is focused on improving privacy and personal comfort in the castle. The great open halls of earlier centuries provided large uncomfortable spaces for communal living, centred around an open fire. In both secular and religious buildings, many of these great spaces were now being partitioned for greater comfort with smaller room and wall fireplaces.

In Durham's great hall Fox reversed Hatfield's policy of enlargement, cutting off the southern end beyond the screens passage and creating four floors of apartments. He may well have done the same at the northern end too. He also rebuilt the kitchen here, against the Norman defences, with two wide stone fireplaces and above them a huge 'breastwork' in brick – its earliest use in Durham.

The adjacent buttery, scullery and brewhouse were all built by 1499, as recorded on the timber-framed partition (25).

In the mid-sixteenth century Bishop Tunstall (1530–59) sought to improve accessibility around the castle, building a new chapel linked to both the north and west ranges by a gallery with new staircase towers at the east and, probably, the west end too. The gallery was a response to the growing fashion for such rooms in the gentry houses and palaces of the period. But it also eased the circulation problems caused by the subdivision of the range into smaller rooms, and its buttressing of the lower walls must have helped stabilise Le Puiset's range which had settled dramatically on its foundations. The chapel was later lengthened by Cosin or Crewe.

Bishop Cosin's 1662 Black Stairs, Durham Castle. (26)

The decline of the castle-palace (1560–1659)

The problem of Durham Castle's military decline must now be considered. Archival and archaeological evidence can help build a picture of the process.

The inner moat next to Palace Green was, in the later medieval period, an anachronism left over from the early Norman days when Palace Green was occupied by the native Saxons, before their expulsion from the castle to the area around the present Market Place. In Owengate this moat was clearly infilled and built upon in the fifteenth century, and at its western end was largely filled up too by the early sixteenth century, much of it with kitchen waste.

In 1603, James VI of Scotland's accession to the English throne signalled the final evaporation of Durham's military role as a border fortress. The castle-palace of the Norman bishops settled into the more sedate role within one of the new kingdom's middle shires.

Little was done to the fabric of the castle in the first half of the seventeenth century. Bishop Neile is said to have erected (or remodelled) the apartments within the north end of the great hall and formed the Senate suite at the east end of the north range (Bishop James' fireplace there was only installed in the 1850s from the old Exchequer).

During the Civil War and the Interregnum, with the bishopric abolished, the castle served as a prison hospital for 500 of the 3000 Scottish prisoners brought from Dunbar after their defeat by Cromwell.

Durham Castle after the Restoration – buildings and gardens (1660–1722)

At the Restoration in 1660, when Bishop John Cosin (1660–72) returned triumphantly to the city, he immediately began work on both his cathedral church and his castle, both much neglected during the Commonwealth. Much of this is recorded in his private correspondence and many of the building contracts survive.

The inadequacies of the medieval castle quickly became apparent to him and, to resolve the cramped circulation between the two main ranges, he commissioned a new staircase, the Black Stairs (**26**). Concealed behind walls that Cosin required to 'answer' Tunstall's stairs, is one of the finest staircases of its time in England, rising through four floors. It is built around a large open well, its balustrades richly carved with Baroque foliage, with a high moulded handrail, easy to grip. The cantilevered stairs eventually settled, leaned inwards and required crude propping to prevent collapse.

The great hall remained Cosin's ceremonial building and he panelled the walls, erected a screen and remodelled Bishop Neile's north end chamber. Outside, he added the classical porch in 1663–4 and encased the medieval buttresses in new stonework, finished with little ogee tops, similar to his chapel at Auckland Castle.

For the first few years of his episcopacy, Durham Castle must have resembled a building site, and around 1664–5, as building work approached completion, Cosin's thoughts turned to the improvements he could make to the external spaces, many of them redundant defences, spaces that an inventive mind might make something of.

Cosin began his landscaping works in 1664, in the courtyard, where he built an oval lead-lined stone fountain. The following year he demolished the cramped medieval barbican, rebuilding it as a generous forecourt, then levelling the adjacent moat for new gardens. Towards the end of

The Bishop's Walk and belvedere tower, Durham Castle, below the cathedral's central tower (from a grisaille painting in the castle, c.1700). (27)

the same year the castle motte beneath Bishop Hatfield's abandoned keep was terraced in three levels, and in early 1666 the walks were turfed and planted with rose trees and gooseberry bushes.

This garden work may have extended to the top of the bastion tower between the castle and the North Gate, which led onto the new North Terrace. The new moat gardens, the present Fellows' and Master's gardens, either side of the barbican, most probably served, respectively, as an orchard and kitchen garden.

One final garden, the Bishop's Walk, is perhaps the most enigmatic and important of all, being well illustrated in contemporary paintings in the castle (**27**). It was established after 1667 and lay to the south west, just below the castle wall. A long terrace walk with formal planting was set out here. Rising above it was a tall octagonal tower with a well-lit upper chamber, aligned on Cosin's new library and looking out over the river below. The vestiges remain of the enclosing walls, the site of the tower acknowledged by the angled

The view of Durham Castle from the cathedral's central tower, showing (right) Bishop Cosin's terraced motte of 1665–6 (from a grisaille painting in the castle, c.1700). (28)

projection of the castle wall. The garden itself survives, just, overgrown and a little neglected, but inviting restoration. This was one of the earliest garden buildings on the peninsula, a belvedere from which to view, not just the narrow Bishop's Walk, but the wider landscape. It was a prescient statement of the direction of future landscaping on the riverbanks.

The Bishop's Walk was probably Cosin's work but it may have been built by his successor Bishop Crewe (1674–1722), who is known to have added a new garden in the castle.[1] Crewe spent much of his long episcopate in Durham and he entertained here on a lavish scale. His new apartments in the Norman Gallery, the enlarged chapel and the extra doors in the lower gallery, all in the north range, may have been a response to the numerous guests who would have stayed. Likewise, his repair of the ruinous keep in 1714 may have been to spare his own blushes by avoiding the risk of falling masonry.

The castle in the Georgian period 1722–1832

Though Durham Castle itself was commodious, it lay within a cramped medieval site, accessible through an equally cramped and insanitary medieval city (**28**). Auckland Castle by comparison was healthier and set within expansive parkland. Little wonder the eighteenth-century bishops increasingly preferred it to Durham. Bishop Butler (1750–2) and his successor Bishop Trevor (1752–71) improved both palaces. At Durham their main work was in the North Range between 1751–6, all under the direction of Sanderson Miller, a well-known designer in the Gothick style.

Miller remodelled and decorated the bishop's dining room, now the Senior Common Room. He inserted two big traceried sash windows deep

into the Norman walls. Bishop Egerton (1771–87) continued the refurbishment in this range, forming the Octagon and refitting the Senate Room with its mid-seventeenth century Flemish tapestries.

These later eighteenth-century bishops, comfortable in their newly improved north range apartments, ignored the increasingly perilous ruins of the long-abandoned Hatfield keep towering over them. Only in 1789 did Bishop Thurlow demolish the upper storeys to make the building safe.

The final embellishment to the episcopal castle was made by Bishop Barrington in 1791, when James Wyatt remodelled the gatehouse, retaining the core of the medieval building. This was the last major building in the castle by the bishops of Durham.

University College (1832–2012)

The new university of 1832 did not occupy the castle immediately. It only became available in 1837 after the death of Bishop Van Mildert, a gap that prompted Anthony Salvin's design (1834) for a new college in the south-west corner of Palace Green. This scheme was abandoned when the castle was available and the work of conversion began, concentrated on the adaptation of the ruined keep for student rooms. Salvin was retained and undertook its rebuilding in 1839–40. His plans and the contractors' tenders clearly indicate that he intended to adapt the existing ruined keep, inserting windows into the medieval walls and refurbishing old staircases. In the event, much was probably rebuilt and certainly the whole exterior stonework was refaced (**29**).

In 1847 the great hall's north window was restored and, in 1882, to commemorate the fiftieth anniversary of the university, it was reglazed in

The keep and Master's House, Durham Castle. (**29**)

stained glass by Kempe. At the same time the hall received its oak panelling and screen, replacing Cosin's original work.

The work in the castle during the last century concentrated on the conservation of the fabric and the sensitive adaptations and adjustments necessary to keep a Norman episcopal castle functioning as a modern university college. Major structural repairs were carried out on the west side of the castle in the 1930s and in 1952 the Norman chapel was restored. By the 1970s additional accommodation was required off site, and Moatside Court (Bernard Taylor & Partners, 1974–7) was neatly inserted into the backlands behind Saddler Street.

A co-ordinated conservation programme began in 1987 with the cleaning of Le Puiset's doorway in the north range, followed by repairs to the gatehouse and north range (north wall). Not that all work was repair. New administrative offices in a minimalist-Tudor style by the castle architect, Dennis Jones, were built in the Fellows' Garden in 1993 (**30**).

Right: *Fellows' Garden building, Durham Castle.* (30)

Below: *Doorcase, Bishop Cosin's Hall, Palace Green.* (31)

Since the Millennium there has been substantial reroofing of the principal ranges, and in 2010–12 major internal renovations were carried out.

Finally, also extensively repaired and redecorated in 2012 is the Master's House, sitting across the former inner moat at the head of Owengate. A tall building, sited along the line of a medieval wall, it dates principally to the early eighteenth century, with finely panelled rooms and staircase, all entered through a side wing of 1712.

PALACE GREEN (EAST SIDE)

The east side of Palace Green begins inauspiciously with public toilets, but these are no ordinary toilets. Standing on Monyers Garth, once the medieval home of the Bishop's mint, they are fashioned out of part of the Bishop's former stables and coach house, designed by Salvin in 1841.[2]

Bailey Court then intervenes, like a newcomer wanting to join in the conversation. This is the most visible edge of a cleverly crafted development in buff brick (for Hatfield College) that weaves its way between North Bailey and Palace Green, a sensitive design for its time (1971, David Roberts).

Bishop Cosin's Hall is a building with great presence, despite being set back. Its appearance suggests an early eighteenth-century date though it may be an earlier building modified. The highlight is its sumptuous doorcase, rich and designed to impress (**31**). Sadly the building's interior fails to live up to its entrance: most has been stripped out, probably due to its changing functions. Originally built as an Archdeacon's Inn, it was briefly a University Hall (hence its name) from 1857 to 1864.

Back on the edge of Palace Green we find Bishop Cosin's Almshouses and Schools (now University Police Office and Almshouses Restaurant). In

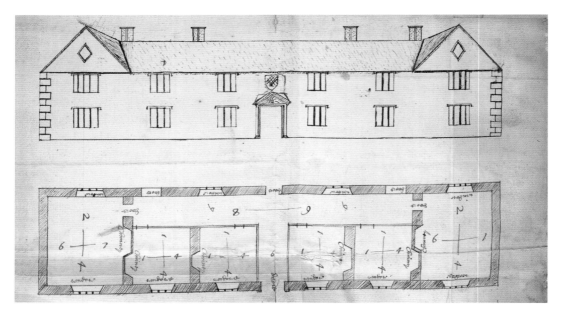

John Longstaffe's drawing of Bishop Cosin's 1668 Almshouses and Schools, Palace Green. (32)

1668 Bishop Cosin rebuilt two earlier Grammar and Song Schools, originally founded by Bishop Langley, as gabled bookends to his new almshouses. The building incorporated earlier medieval fabric in its rear wall and was built as drawn by Cosin's master mason, John Longstaffe, except for the substitution of a more appropriately modest Tudor doorway (**32**). It is a little emasculated now, shorn of its chimney stacks and its interior gutted when it was converted to a museum in 1876, at which time most windows were renewed.[3]

The Pemberton Building of 1931 need not detain us long.[4] Containing lecture rooms, and former Union Society premises, it was designed by WD Caroe in a cold stone, but respectful of its setting and adding some interest.

Abbey House (Department of Theology) is a well-documented building that creeps, stage left, into many a panorama of its larger neighbour (**33**). A late seventeenth-century brick house incorporating medieval fragments – see an arched doorway in Dun Cow Lane – it originally sported fine curved and patterned brick gables, best seen with a strained neck in the alley beside its north wall. Early the following century its Palace Green front was refaced in ashlar, along with new panelled rooms and a staircase. It formerly had fine gate piers and a neat front garden, all gone for simplicity and a well-concealed sub-station, but surely still capable of a little re-greening?

Abbey House, Palace Green. (33)

MUSIC SCHOOL

The University's Music School sits on the edge of the cathedral cemetery, with its rear wall in Windy Gap rising from the bedrock. In 1541, after the dissolution of the cathedral priory and the establishment of the Dean and Chapter, a Grammar School was founded there, built, it is said, on the site of the Bishop's medieval tithe barn – there are earlier footings in the north wall. In 1661 Bishop Cosin rebuilt it, or more likely raised it, lighting the eastern schoolroom, overlooking Palace Green with his characteristic Gothic window (**34**). The western half was the schoolmaster's house and this was improved in the early eighteenth century, retaining its original doorway, inside are a seventeenth-century staircase and finely panelled rooms. In the schoolroom, its roof still supported on Cosin's upper cruck trusses, generations of schoolboys have carved their names in the dado panelling. The whole building was restored in 1844 by cathedral architect, George Pickering. A western extension was added in 1899 and in 1966 it was converted to the Music School (Bernard Taylor & Partners).

Music School, Palace Green. (34)

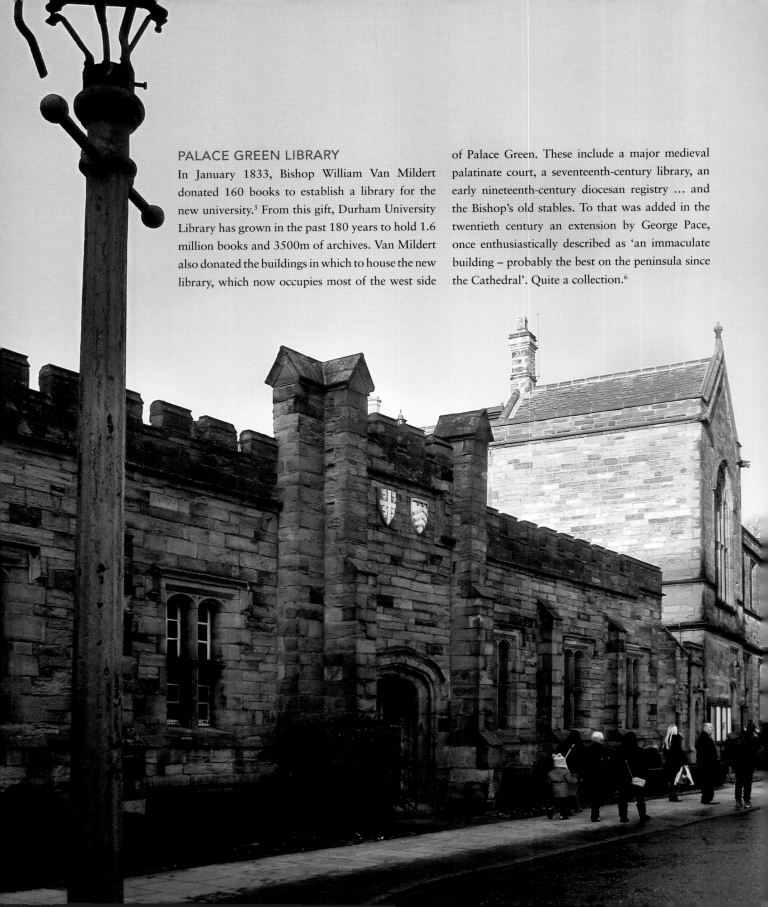

PALACE GREEN LIBRARY

In January 1833, Bishop William Van Mildert donated 160 books to establish a library for the new university.[5] From this gift, Durham University Library has grown in the past 180 years to hold 1.6 million books and 3500m of archives. Van Mildert also donated the buildings in which to house the new library, which now occupies most of the west side of Palace Green. These include a major medieval palatinate court, a seventeenth-century library, an early nineteenth-century diocesan registry … and the Bishop's old stables. To that was added in the twentieth century an extension by George Pace, once enthusiastically described as 'an immaculate building – probably the best on the peninsula since the Cathedral'. Quite a collection.[6]

Above: *The northern half of Palace Green Library with Bishop Cosin's Library (centre) and the Exchequer (right).* (35)

Opposite: *The southern half of Palace Green Library with the Old Diocesan Registry of 1820.* (36)

Right: *Exhibition spaces in the new interior of Palace Green Library.* (37)

A summary history

The new University Library began in Bishop Cosin's Library, and it was there Van Mildert added a gallery and stair turret (1834) designed by Anthony Salvin (35). During the 1850s three major bequests and donations necessitated expansion into 'Little Cosin' and the adjacent Exchequer building, to the north. By 1857 some of the Bishop's stables, south of Cosin's Library had been adapted to lecture rooms for the teaching of Greek and Mathematics but, in 1882, these were demolished for new lecture rooms and a large hall, designed by Sir Arthur Blomfield.[7]

By 1929 the Exchequer Library was overflowing with books and the large ground-floor lecture room, below Blomfield's main hall, was incorporated into the library. This building was still separated from the old library by the Bishop's carriage drive from Palace Green to the former stables and so a passageway was built, still surviving as the corridor behind Cosin's Library, giving entry into Little Cosin. This gap was finally closed in when a new library entrance was created in 1935–7, designed by Caröe & Passmore.

By the early 1950s the whole of the old Bishop's stables and coach-houses had been incorporated into the library, one range having been earlier converted into a Fives Court. Oscar Faber's 1950s scheme finally covered in the old open yard of the former stables, linking with surrounding ranges. In 1961 the garden in the SW corner of the library, now cleared of huts, was chosen for the major extension designed by George Pace.[8] In 1978 the Old Registry, later Union Society, was incorporated into the library (36).[9]

Blomfield's main first-floor lecture hall was later converted to a library, later still into an exhibition space. The whole library has recently undergone a major repair and reordering scheme including new exhibition space, to be completed in 2014 (Harrogate Design Group/Howarth Litchfield Partnership/GSS Architecture – architects John Edwards and John Dutton) (37).

Exchequer

The Exchequer's name is a little misleading, as it housed a number of the bishop's officers including, in the long first-floor room, the Chancery Court. It is a very important building in Durham's history – a rare medieval court building, the last survivor of the medieval bishops' offices that once lined Palace Green, and the repository for some of the most precious books in the University Library.

The building's original circulation pattern is still uncertain because later alterations have destroyed much of the evidence. What is certain is that it was originally entered centrally from Palace Green between vaulted basement rooms, along a passage that once led to a narrow spiral staircase, or possibly to a straight stone flight of stairs, either of which delivered the visitor to the first floor. This straight flight has also been credited to Bishop Cosin, but, whatever its date, it was removed when the Palace Green access was closed in 1935. On the first floor is a fine rib-vaulted lobby, off which all rooms are reached (**38**). To the left, a tall arched doorway, still with its medieval door in place, led through to offices, while on the right, two basket-arched doorways led into the Chancery Court. On both sides, the rooms still retain their moulded-beamed ceilings (**39**).

The courtroom was formally laid out, with seats and a table for the Chancellor, Registrar and barristers. Beyond, probably kept apart by a low screen, were the public.[10] Each – officers and public – probably had their own doorway, as there are now two doors into one space.

From the first-floor lobby, another spiral stair originally rose to the second floor, but this was most probably rendered redundant by Cosin's improvements in 1668, when he inserted a more generous dog-leg staircase, parts of which were incorporated into the present pre-1837 stair.[11] The second floor rooms also retain their original ceiling beams, though most of their fireplaces now lie behind the library shelving.

The Exchequer building was originally lit by small pairs of trefoil-headed lancet windows – a curiously archaic design for the mid-fifteenth century – but most of the external fenestration is

Left: *Vaulted lobby on the first floor of the Exchequer, Palace Green.* (38)

Below: *Interior of the Exchequer, Palace Green.* (39)

Above: *The Exchequer from Fellows' Garden, Palace Green.* (40)

Right: *Bishop John Cosin (1660–72).* (41)

now in the form of Cosin's large triple-light late Gothic designs, many of which were added in 1855 when the building was restored (**40**).

Bishop Cosin's Library

John Cosin arrived in Durham in 1624 as Bishop Neile's chaplain, canon of Durham Cathedral and rector of Brancepeth and Elwick. As a high Anglican member of a largely like-minded chapter, he was influential in promoting the church reforms advocated by Archbishop Laud throughout the Diocese of Durham (**41**). In 1634 he became Master of Peterhouse, Cambridge, later Vice-Chancellor there in 1639 and Dean of Peterborough in 1640. In 1644, deprived of all preferments by the Long Parliament, he fled into exile to Paris, where he became Anglican chaplain at the court of Charles I's widow, Henrietta Maria.

After the Restoration of Charles II in 1660, John Cosin returned home to Durham as bishop until his death in 1672. During this period he was the major influence in the repair and restoration of the cathedral, his episcopal palaces at Durham and Auckland castles, and the refurnishing of his diocesan churches. Back in Durham he also found a final home for his library in the building that bears his name.

Cosin had a great love of books. His first church appointment was as chaplain and librarian to John Overall, then Bishop of Lichfield.[12] In Durham, in 1628, he was instrumental in drawing up an Act of the Durham Chapter to 'replenish and maintain' the cathedral library. He also amassed his own collection, and when forced into exile he sent almost 1200 books to his old college at Cambridge for safekeeping. With Cosin back in Durham in 1660, his books returned too, and in September 1661 they were being kept in the long gallery at Auckland Castle.[13] This was only a temporary home, as Cosin planned a purpose-built library on Palace Green. Unusually for a man noted for recording his own generosity, no foundation documents survive, but the building was completed in 1668.

The design and building of the library is almost certainly the work of John Longstaffe of Bishop Auckland, Cosin's favoured mason, who worked on many of his buildings notably at Auckland Castle, and the County Court and Almshouses on Palace Green in Durham. Longstaffe was a fervent Quaker and it sheds a light on Cosin's character that as a high Anglican, fundamentally at odds with Quakerism, the bishop was nevertheless tolerant enough to employ him, time and again, as his mason. The

relationship becomes even more remarkable, when Longstaffe was being fined in the bishop's own court for holding a Quaker meeting at his home, in the same period as he is being paid by him for services rendered – what he received from Cosin in one hand, he repaid to him with the other.

Cosin's Library is a rectangular hall of coursed sandstone. Its original appearance was a little less stolid than now, having once had a flat lead roof and a crenellated parapet, replaced with a high-pitched roof and a plain parapet in the later nineteenth century.[14] The original entrance was in the middle of the east wall, through a fine classical doorway, its pediment split open to make room for Cosin's essential signature – his coat of arms. The single room within is lit by high three-light basket-arched windows, on all sides except the west, where a large, full-height, five-light window fills the wall. The library's original east elevation, its public face to Palace Green, thus contains the quintessential Cosin ingredients of both classical (doorway) and Gothic (parapet and windows) motifs in one façade. It is the same stylistic mix that appears on many of his buildings, notably the castle.

Once inside, through a small lobby, the rich interior of the library woodwork would have greeted the visitor. The internal layout of the bookcases was clearly a matter for Cosin rather than Longstaffe. Setting the shelving *against* the walls, rather than in bookshelves at right angles to them in the English fashion, was an innovative layout based on continental models. It had been introduced into England in the early seventeenth century in the Arts End of the Bodleian Library at Oxford, but Cosin's library was possibly the

first substantial new English library to be designed on that principle.[15] Cosin, no doubt, chose this layout based on his knowledge of the French examples, notably the Bibliothèque Mazarine in Paris. Originally the double-bookcases were to be separated by readers' seats, but even within his lifetime they had to be infilled with more bookcases as his library grew. The original bookcases were painted in a matt buff colour, though their doors may be later additions (**42**).

Above each double bookcase, painted on an oblong canvas panel, were three portraits, representing the authors whose books appeared on the shelves below. This was a feature already seen in England (at the Bodleian) and abroad, and Cosin employed his painter/artist Jan Baptist Van Eersell to carry out the work. Van Eersell was more often found painting Cosin's woodwork elsewhere in 'shadow' and 'trail' work and, let us be kind here, did not take naturally to portraiture. Bishop Cosin found the results 'ugly and unworthy of the room', telling his painter to rework the images. It is far from clear whether he ever did this, as he left Durham shortly after, never, it seems, to return.

With a growing library collection, Cosin's final improvement was to commission Longstaffe to build a small additional room – now called Little Cosin – in the gap between the new library and the Exchequer, and to instruct his joiners to build the furnishings for it. It was completed in 1671 but the planned portraits above the bookshelves, continuing the work in the main library, had to wait until 1961–2, when the then University Librarian, David Ramage, undertook the work. It is unclear when the two rooms above Little Cosin were built – were they done by Cosin or added later?

The tall proportions of the main library have prompted the suggestion that Cosin may have intended a gallery to be provided, but this is unlikely; more probably he hung paintings there.[16] His successors did little in the building and it was left to Bishop Van Mildert to provide a gallery in 1834 along with a new entrance turret. Warden Thorp also had the north wall fireplace inserted. In 1991, the library stock totalled 4400 volumes of which three-quarters came from Cosin or his time.[17]

In recent years, despite a 1950s restoration,[18] the discovery of dampness beneath the library floor prompted the temporary removal of its contents. A major project was undertaken to repair the building, conserve the fabric of the interior and create the environmental conditions that would enable the return of the books. This work was completed in 2012 under the direction of the library's Head of Conservation, Liz Branigan, with woodwork repair and conservation by Bob Elsey. Now, perhaps for the first time in centuries, the warmth of the library's beautiful woodwork can be fully appreciated.

The Pace building, Palace Green, from Broken Walls. (43)

Pace Library

George Pace was already a highly respected architect when the university commissioned him to design the library extension in 1961. His York practice was almost exclusively known for its church work, mostly Anglican churches in the North of England and Wales. His work embraced the conservation of historic churches as well as the design of new ones, and he had that rare talent of being very good at both. His work in Durham dates from his appointment as cathedral architect in 1954. He also worked for the university since 1958, when his first job was to design the light fittings for Bishop Cosin's Library.[19]

The library extension site was an intimidating one. On plan it looks to be to the rear of the main Palace Green Library, ie away from the frontage, concealed. But in Durham, of course, there is no 'rear', rarely is there anywhere to hide. The extension site was set between castle and cathedral, central in the peninsula's main panorama – its principal façade – viewed from South Street.

Into this great view, Pace added a remarkable building, completed in 1966. Five storeys high with a double-height library over three floors of book stacks, it had a concrete frame with stone walls and lead roofs, articulated towards the river by a bastion tower of a staircase just where one might have been, above the castle walls. The defensive theme continued in the slit-windowed treatment of much of the library's blank walling (**43**). The library extension was built higher than approved, and subsequently, after great debate, six

feet were taken off the rooftop service room by way of an honourable compromise.

The external stonework of the main façade is executed in local sandstone rubble, though not traditionally coursed rubble (not remotely coursed at all in fact), but rather an intentionally irregular pattern, which upsets many who see it. It might be an unforgivable blemish were it not exquisitely executed, complemented by beautiful ashlar work and slate damp-proof course. Away from such public gaze, up Windy Gap, for example, Pace reverts to much shuttered concrete in an honestly twentieth-century manner.

Internally the principal space is the library, with its double-height vista, through a great mullioned and transomed glazed screen, out to the riverbank trees. The library has a central well, surrounded by the gallery, a space, reminiscent to Elain Harwood, of Mackintosh's library at the Glasgow School of Art.[20] But Pace then plays a trick to jolt what might have been the orthogonal restfulness of the interior. Over the library, the ceiling rooflights are set diagonally in a grid, which owes something to earlier examples by Le Corbusier in Paris, and Powell & Moya's work at Brasenose College, Oxford, a building Pace is known to have admired (**44**). Local exemplars were also cited by Pace himself when he wrote

the roof of the Prior's Kitchen and the silhouette of the Castle, the chimney stacks of the Deanery and the now demolished great gateway of the Castle (North Gate), are some of the local motifs from which the spirit has been distilled.

The result is a triumph.

Interior, Pace building, Palace Green Library. (44)

THE PENINSULA:
THE BAILEY

SETTING

Over the years, the university has expanded south, beyond its initial endowment around Palace Green and North Bailey, to take in almost all of the Bailey houses. They were home to those, past and present, who served the cathedral's prior, dean and bishop. Gentry families that once garrisoned the castle kept their houses into more peaceful times, lawyers who advised the Chapter lived close by, and more humble craftsmen who laboured for them, all lived here (**45**).

The university's presence in the Bailey now focuses on four colleges – Hatfield, St Chad's, St John's and St Cuthbert's. In none of them will you find a traditional college quad, fully enclosed by buildings. In each college, one side is open to a different prospect, the cathedral or the riverbank landscape.

General view of the Bailey, looking north from College Gate. (45)

OWENGATE

Owengate, which rises and twists to reveal the cathedral panorama, is one of Durham's most visually exciting streets, if one of its shortest. (**46**). In medieval times it was enclosed by the great North Gate at the bottom and a further gate at the top. Its north side was, at first, part of the castle moat, but by the fifteenth century that had been infilled and built over.

No 2 was largely rebuilt after the demolition of the adjacent North Gate in 1820, its narrow rear wing still sitting on top of the medieval castle wall, adjacent to the ruined fourteenth-century bastion, inserted between motte and gate.

Nos 3–6 Owengate, with other North Bailey properties, were central to the 1950s debate between the university, the local authorities and objectors, about how extensive the clearance of historic buildings should be to provide new student accommodation. Architects came and went, and development opportunities in New Elvet relieved some of the pressure. When work finally began in the early 1960s it was in the careful hands of architect David Roberts from Cambridge. His sensitive approach to retention and conversion, alongside some infilling of new building, was a great success, even if, by today's standards, there were some casualties.

Owengate. (46)

No 3 is, in origin, a group of three medieval buildings, the roof of the front one reassembled complete at a higher level when the house was altered and raised *c*.1700. No 4 is a much simpler late eighteenth-century affair, but No 5's late medieval origin is evident in its jettied first floor (**47**).[1] Its neighbour at No 6 is another late eighteenth-century house with older rear.[2]

Opposite, Bishop Cosin's Almshouses, rebuilt here in 1838 to replace those on Palace Green given to the new university, have now been splendidly converted to a World Heritage Centre.[3] Next door is the former New Exchequer Building of 1851, built to house the palatinate manuscript records displaced from the Old Exchequer, when it became the Library.[4] It was designed by George Pickering in a rather heavy Gothic, but it turns the corner well.[5]

NORTH BAILEY HOUSES

Most of the North Bailey houses described here formed part of the original bequest to the new university in 1832. Hatfield College grew out of that and, further south, gradual acquisitions and transfers led to the establishment of St Chad's College, St John's College and St Cuthbert's Society.

The remaining non-collegiate houses are now largely in departmental use. They share those same characteristics that can be seen in Owengate, in all the Bailey colleges and in Old Elvet – historic buildings with an outward appearance of one date, often masking an interior of a much earlier period. This reflects not only the understandable human trait of presenting a good face, but also underlies the limited wealth of Durham citizens, that allowed for improvement but only rarely funded complete rebuilding of their homes.

No 5 Owengate – a rare late-medieval survival. (47)

On the east side, 1 and 2 North Bailey (St Chad's College and Music) and Queen's Court are early nineteenth-century buildings, no doubt replacing those affected, or possibly damaged, by the demolition of the adjacent North Gate in 1820.

Much further down the east side is 24 North Bailey, occupied by the Union Society (**48**). Once

No 24 North Bailey. (48)

two houses, its southern half is a late seventeenth-century building, its northern neighbour a remodelling of *c*.1760 to present the visitor with a spectacular entrance hall with a large Venetian window, lighting a fine open-well staircase.

Right: *Staircase, 46 North Bailey.* (49)

Below right: *The exterior of the Assembly Rooms, North Bailey.* (50)

Returning north, on the west side after Dun Cow Lane, come 38 and 39 North Bailey (Department of Classics). No 38 is essentially a late seventeenth-century house, with older fabric in the rear wall of the front range and possibly in the rear wing too. It has an added second floor and a later eighteenth-century façade. No 39 has an early eighteenth-century front, with older fabric, such as the heavy ceiling beams, behind.

Then comes the 1971 Hatfield College rebuilding by David Roberts (Nos 41 and 42), also cleverly stitching new student rooms into the narrow space between the Bailey and Palace Green. Next is the 1958 rebuilding of No 43 by the same architect (with Charles Elgey), also reusing doorcases from the demolished properties.

Nos 44–46 North Bailey (Department of History) are two houses. Nos 44–45 is a late seventeenth-century building, but the heavily beamed front room in No 45 could be earlier. The façades have been remodelled much later. No 46 may have an early seventeenth–century front range with a new staircase added about a century later (**49**).

The last house on this side of the street is No 49, actually a pair of houses, the southern early eighteenth century, the northern all nineteenth century in date.

ASSEMBLY ROOMS

There is usually no better use for an historic building than that for which it was built. So it is such a delight to see Durham Student Theatre still performing in the same, newly refurbished, space as their eighteenth-century predecessors (**50**). Probably dating from the middle of that century, the Assembly Rooms were the centre of entertainment for Durham's fashionable society, who would gather there for concerts, balls and parties. Larger dramas and plays were staged nearby in the Georgian theatres off Saddler Street. The auditorium retains its original panelling, overmantel and modillion cornice (**51**).

By the end of the nineteenth century the Assembly Rooms were in decline, and in 1891 new owners carried out major internal alterations.[6] The narrow Bailey façade retains work of this period on its first floor, which sits above a more modern entrance of 1949–50.[7]

HATFIELD COLLEGE

The second college of the university lies in an enviable position in North Bailey. Its main courtyard is set on a steep slope, enclosed on three sides, but partially open to the street, closure provided by the wonderful bulk of the cathedral's

east end. Add to this an unusual site history, quite unlike anything else in the city, and Hatfield's buildings command attention. Were that not sufficient reason to explore, it also has two of the most elegant rooms on the Durham peninsula.

Beginnings

In 1843 the university bought a North Bailey property belonging to a Durham solicitor, Mr Scruton, and in 1846 it became Bishop Hatfield's Hall.[8] David Melville, its first Principal, disliked the rich living style of castle students and proposed a cheaper domestic college life for students of more limited means.[9] The Hatfield model was to let furnished rooms, with all meals taken in the hall, and students charged a fixed price for board and lodgings. Students and staff were to be regarded as members of one community. This new system was very influential and became the norm for Durham colleges, and also later at Oxford and Cambridge.[10] Hatfield became a college in 1919.

The castle wall, D Stairs and the dining hall

Hatfield College sits on top of the castle wall, which here as elsewhere around the peninsula is of many periods, being an important retaining wall always in need of repair. But there is medieval work in its lower sections, though most of the buttresses are relatively recent *(see **186**)*. The large medieval relieving arch near the gate is enigmatic and may have been to carry the wall over unstable ground, a structural solution used further north, near the site of the North Gate.

Mr Scruton's house was unique on the Bailey, rising off this wall rather than along the street frontage, The forecourt, thus created, was vast compared to the pinched proportions of many of

Left: *Mid-eighteenth-century decorative plasterwork, Assembly Rooms, North Bailey.* (51)

A detail of Bok's panorama of the city from Whinney Hill (probably c.1665) showing the large crenellated house, set on the castle wall, now part incorporated into D Stairs, Hatfield College. (52)

the gentry houses along the street. So who lived there?

At least the building's recent history is well known – it had begun life as a private house, but in 1760 it became a coaching inn, in 1783 known as the Red Lion,[11] but by 1799 it had reverted to a private house.[12] But early maps and peninsular panoramas show these buildings against the castle wall as far back as the mid-seventeenth century. Could an older, medieval family have established this unusual layout?[13]

From at least 1642 to 1660 the house was owned by John Heath IV, one of a gentry family who first lived at Kepier Hospital, just north of the city.[14] While he was living on the Bailey, John Heath was laying out his great garden at Old Durham, just east of the city, moving there in the 1640s, dying in 1665.

In that same year an unknown artist, V. Bok, drew a detailed panorama of Durham from Whinney Hill (**52**). Included is Heath's old house, part still standing as D Stairs. It is a remarkable survival, though much disguised by later alterations.

Bok's view shows a large crenellated building, three storeys high over a basement. It appears to have occupied the length of the two rooms south of the college's dining hall – the Senior Common Room's (SCR) dining and sitting room. The thick walls and low beamed ceiling of the sitting room, together with the surviving (if part renewed) mullioned window in the castle wall below, are all of this period. The adjacent SCR dining room was later raised and given a shallow curved bay window in the late eighteenth century with a ceiling plastered with delicate Adamish fluting (53).

The seventeenth-century house was probably one room deep and the small patch of rendered wall visible from the quad is probably the remains of its projecting entrance porch or stair tower. The surrounding mid-eighteenth-century brickwork is a widening of the building to improve circulation between floors and rooms. It has a fine dogleg staircase, with running 'Durham' string, and must represent the adaptation of the private house to a coaching inn.

In the bedroom of Mr Scruton's house stood a large early seventeenth-century fireplace, with overmantel portraits of Stuart royalty. This was specifically excluded from the sale to the university, destined instead to grace the Old Council Chamber in the Town Hall, where it can still be seen.

At right angles to the old house lies the main dining hall, one of Durham's finest college halls, still, like the castle hall, used for the purpose it was built 250 years ago. It must be an addition, built after 1760 when the house became a coaching inn, but it was also used for public music recitals. It is a handsome, well-proportioned room, with a coved ceiling and a beautifully detailed Venetian east window (54).

Top: *The dining room of the Senior Common Room, Hatfield College.* (53)

Above: *The dining hall of Hatfield College.* (54)

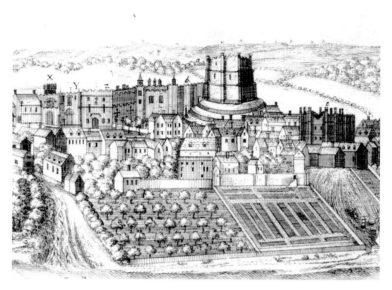

Early Gardens

As the dining hall and SCR dining room windows demonstrate, the position of the house lent itself to riverbank views. Given John Heath IV's green-fingered pedigree – his family built large gardens at Kepier, as he did at Old Durham – it is highly likely he laid out the riverbanks below the castle wall as a formal terraced garden, possibly one of the earliest on the peninsula. The banks there were certainly cultivated in 1723, when Samuel Buck drew an eastern prospect of the city (**55**), and by the mid-nineteenth century they were laid out as an orchard.[15] Early photographs show a symmetrical double-ramped stone retaining wall mid-slope, probably indicative of a formal garden (**56**).

Above: *Detail of Samuel Buck's panorama of Durham, c.1723, showing an orchard and gardens on the riverbanks below the present Hatfield College.* (55)

Right: *An early twentieth-century view of Hatfield College, showing evidence of formal gardens with its symmetrically ramped retaining wall, aligned on the D Stairs building above.* (56)

Nineteenth–century college improvements

With the establishment of Hatfield Hall, it quickly became apparent that more student rooms were needed. Anthony Salvin's A and B Stairs (Melville Building) were completed in 1849 in a sober Jacobean style and have 24 rooms around two staircases (**57**). The quad façade is the plainer of the two main elevations, though, whether by accident or design (for the range risked overstepping its boundary), the projection forward of the southernmost rooms very effectively terminates the run of buildings along the east side of the quad.

In 1853 the chapel was built, designed in a Decorated Gothic style by Revd James Francis Turner, chaplain of Bishop Cosin's Hall, later Bishop of Grafton and Armidale (**58**).[16] Before entering the priesthood, Turner was architect-trained, studying under Philip Hardwick, designer of London's Euston Station and, more locally, Durham Town Hall. The fall of the land eastwards required the chapel's east end to be supported on basement arches, a delightful feature developed into a covered footpath when the college later expanded northwards *(see 185)*. Inside the chapel, the slender scissor-braced roof trusses are noteworthy, one of them supported on corbels fashioned as heads of Bishop Van Mildert and probably Warden Thorp.[17] Later furnishings were added 1859–76,[18] but the reredos and Harrison organ on its west gallery date from 1883, designed by architect Charles Hodgson Fowler.

The Rectory

Increased student numbers towards the end of the nineteenth century led to expansion on all sides. No 7 North Bailey, or Jevons House, to the north, became the Principal's House, while houses across

Above: *A and B Stairs, Hatfield College.* (57)

Left: *Detail of the woodwork in the chapel, Hatfield College.* (58)

Above right: *The interior of the Birley Room in the Rectory, Hatfield College, probably once the dining room with a buffet beyond the columns.* (59)

the street at 41 and 42 North Bailey, also became Hatfield property. In 1894/5, the college acquired the so-called Rectory building that lay to the south, though in fact it had only served that purpose for 24 years at the end of the eighteenth century.[19]

Much has been made of the Rectory's great antiquity.[20] If there is an older structure concealed, there is no evidence in its plan – no inexplicably thick walls. Rather what is evident, and very good, is of the later eighteenth century – a delightful oval entrance hall with Gothic blind arcading, a well staircase of plain balusters interspersed with ornate ironwork (very rare in Durham) and best of all, the Birley Room (**59**). This is a superb panelled dining room with a large semicircular bay window. The room is entered through an anteroom, once the buffet servery, divided from the main room by slender quatrefoil columns with leaf capitals. There is nothing here of the lavish carving and plasterwork

of the slightly earlier Tristram Room at St John's College, just commendable self-restraint – cool and elegant – proof, as always, that 'less is more'.

Twentieth century

The twentieth century bestowed mixed blessings on Hatfield. Salvin designed his A and B Stairs to be extended northwards, but that only took place when W T Jones's C Stairs were built in 1931–3. The style was inoffensive neo-Georgian, its façade to the riverbanks terrace encasing the base of the castle wall. The year 1950 saw gains and losses. The university installed the peninsula's district-heating boiler house against the Bailey, sterilising that end of the quad – its forthcoming removal can only offer great opportunities to the college. Far better was Vincent Harris's Pace Building (E, F, G and H Stairs), set in the gardens of Jevons House – essentially an early eighteenth-century revival with fine stonework, powerful façades and steep roofs with a nice interplay of two dormer designs (**60**).

In 1956 the old gatehouse was demolished, after partially collapsing, revealing the foundations of earlier medieval structures.[21] The new gatehouse that followed (1961–3) provided student rooms and offices wrapped in uneventful Georgian vernacular, designed by Thomas Worthington & Sons, the architects of Grey College.[22]

If the 1950s had given Hatfield revivalist and traditional buildings, Bernard Taylor & Partners' rebuilding of the ancient Jevons House in 1966–9 brought the college up to date. It presented the same wall-like façade to the Bailey as Jevons had done and tried quite successfully, in pale modern brick, to interpret traditional forms in a contemporary manner.

ST CHAD'S COLLEGE

St Chad's College is not what it seems. Like its neighbours St John's and St Cuthbert's, behind the separate façades of many Bailey houses there is a single university college. In all three, the deception works magnificently. But it might not have been so at Chad's. Its saviour was Francis Johnson, a brilliant classicist architect, swimming against the prevailing tide of twentieth-century modernists. His appreciation of the individuality of each house, and his particular love of its staircases, served Chad's well. But the college is not all about its buildings; behind them lie its gardens. Once they were some of the most historically puzzling on the peninsula, but now perhaps the best set on the Bailey, still with surprises in store.

The Pace building, Hatfield College. (60)

History

First established in Hooton Pagnall, near Doncaster, St Chad's Hall was opened as a theological college in 1904 at 1 South Bailey with 19 students training for the Anglican priesthood. It became an independent college within the university in 1919, and as its numbers grew over the following decades, so its members were soon taking a variety of non-theological degrees. The college ceased training for the priesthood in 1972.

From its South Bailey base, the college expanded first into 28 North Bailey, then into property on Palace Green and Dun Cow Lane.[23] Further North Bailey houses were acquired and in 1930 the original South Bailey house was extended. But by then much of the college's centre of gravity had moved northwards to its present site, beneath the cathedral, and later house-swapping with other colleges consolidated that position.

1930s rebuilding

In 1934 the college first embraced the idea of a new college building to replace its disparate collection of houses.[24] London architect Leslie T Moore's design would have been dour and overbearing on any site, but given the college's position, closer than any other to one of the world's great buildings, with hindsight it seems inconceivable that it would ever have been built (**61**). By good fortune the college's Council was reporting in 1938 that there were still inadequate funds to make a start. The Second World War put pay to thoughts of any further work and in the post-war austerity years nothing was done.

Francis Johnson

In 1956 the college dusted off the Moore scheme and planned to start building. But in the intervening

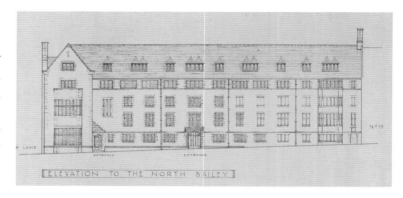

ELEVATION TO THE NORTH BAILEY

The Leslie T Moore 1930s scheme for a new St Chad's College. (61)

two decades, times had changed. Thomas Sharp's 1944 report on Durham, *Cathedral City – A Plan For Durham*, declared the peninsular precincts of the castle and cathedral to be sacrosanct. Moore's scheme also came in for some influential criticism from the Society for the Protection of Ancient Buildings. The college paused, took stock and started again. The following year it approached four new architects, amongst them Francis Johnson. He had previously worked for his relation, H L Hicks, who had been the college's architect up to his death in 1948. Johnson was also recommended by College Council member Canon George Addleshaw, who knew Johnson's close friend, Edward Ingram. Johnson was duly appointed.

St Chad's was to be Johnson's largest commission.[25] He must have recoiled at the Moore proposal, preferring instead to stitch any new buildings into the Bailey with as little disruption as possible to the grain of the street – its organic character of individual houses, a strong vertical emphasis, and a broadly similar constraint on building height. In this task he worked closely with Thomas Sharp, who had been retained by the City Council as an advisor. They worked well together, Johnson saying of Sharp that he was 'the finest town-planner I have ever been associated with'.

Francis Johnson's final scheme (1961–3) has been hailed as 'a pioneer demonstration of urban conservation', a very rare thing in the early 1960s.[26] He would retain the fabric of the old houses as much as possible, in depth in places, one room deep nearer Bow Lane, where he wholly replaced dilapidated menial buildings with a new college dining hall, kitchens and student rooms above (**62**). Behind the street frontage he created a courtyard with new buildings containing common rooms. (The courtyard was successfully glazed over by Amdega in 2003 (**63**)).[27] Johnson's dining

Below: *The Bailey frontages of St Chad's College.* (62)

Right: *The covered courtyard, St Chad's College.* (63)

hall sits easily on the Bailey, yet is distinctive in its own right. The front has a gentle convex curve, faced with a light brown brick to reflect the cathedral stone opposite. Inside, the dining hall has arched windows of intersecting glazing bars and a plaster-vaulted ceiling, actually a panel of almost German Baroque curved outline, floating beneath the structural ceiling, concealing the ventilation and lighting (64).

Elsewhere the classicism is less apparent and the colonnade to the garden quite contemporary in appearance. The garden elevation is particularly well articulated – handling a long block, with a sense of the individual gabled façades characteristic of the backs of Bailey houses (65). The central gable is off centre, a suitably organic position in the composition, one might think, until it lines up perfectly with the cathedral's Nine Altars gable and the central tower behind, so Johnson intended that students unwittingly would be walking down the cathedral axis when they entered their garden. A clever trick.

The historic houses and their staircases

The college stretches from the corner of Bow Lane, 15 North Bailey, to Nos 22/22A North Bailey. Outlying buildings include 25 North Bailey, Principal's Lodge, Dun Cow Lane and 1 North Bailey. A selection of the best features of these buildings is offered.

No 16 North Bailey has been largely incorporated into the Johnson scheme, though it retains its front rooms to the Bailey.

No 17, however, extends back its full depth and now forms the southern flank of the enclosed courtyard. Despite its later eighteenth-century Bailey façade, like so many Durham houses it

masks earlier fabric. Early documents (c.1604) refer to three tenements here having been combined into one house, and this plan may survive in its long length.[28] The side doorway into the courtyard is late seventeenth century, its door probably a little older. It has a very fine dogleg staircase, with unusual alternate baluster designs, dating from early in the following century. Francis Johnson added the ground-floor rear bay.

There are two No 18s! No 18 (North) dates from the early eighteenth century, but was altered in the Victorian era. Francis Johnson redesigned the rear gable and added a ground floor bay. No 18 (South) has an eighteenth-century front and back, but within is a handsome late seventeenth-century staircase with the single bine twist balusters that were popular after the Restoration.

Two No 19s too! No 19 (North), part of Lightfoot House, is a mid-eighteenth-century house with a fine contemporary staircase, despite being rearranged in part. Well staircases allow for

Above: *Francis Johnson's dining hall at St Chad's College.* (64)

Previous pages: *Francis Johnson's additions behind St Chad's College's Bailey houses, with the garden entrance on the cathedral's main axis.* (65)

greater architectural display than the narrower dogleg stairs, and this example, with its delicate balusters and sweeping handrail, ramped at each turn, is particularly appealing (**74**). No 19 (South), part of Lightfoot House, is a modest house by Bailey standards and may be entirely of early nineteenth century date.

No 20, the third part of Lightfoot House, is yet another complex building. Its eighteenth-century front sash windows belie its façade's late seventeenth-century date, built of narrow brick, with moulded string courses and, hidden behind the gutter, cogged eaves brickwork. Inside is a perfect mid-eighteenth-century dogleg stair with beautifully fluted newel posts and a panelled dado following the line of the handrail.

No 21 appears to have an early eighteenth-century façade resashed later in the century.

The late seventeenth-century staircase, 22 North Bailey, St Chad's College. (66)

Documents in the 1690s refer to it as 'Blew posts' probably a reference to its old timber-framed façade.[29] Its rear brick elevation, of paired sashes between projecting strings, with tumbled-in brickwork in the gable is particularly complete and very attractive. It has almost an Amsterdam air about it, and must date from around 1700. Inside it has a single flight of a later eighteenth-century staircase, perhaps reset.

Nos 22 and 22A were originally two houses but were refaçaded, and converted into one house by the new owner, Samuel Castle, in 1796 *(see front rainwater pipe)*. The main doorcase has curiously fluted and turned columns. Inside (No 22), to the rear, an impressive late seventeenth-century staircase survives in its upper flights, complete with ball finials on its newel posts (**66**). The lower flights have been restored in the nineteenth century but with some gusto and quality, introducing diabolo balusters to the composition. On adjoining walls are *ex situ* console brackets of seventeenth century date, of some quality – where can they be from? Inside 22A is the upper portion only of a small late seventeenth-century well staircase, but a very fine one, with a pulvinated (swollen) closed string with a carved dentil course *(see 72)*.

No 25 North Bailey stands a little apart from the other college buildings further down the Bailey. It is worthy of special mention because of its relative completeness, exterior and interior. It dates from around 1820, and its Bailey frontage has a particularly attractive doorcase, round-arched with door and fanlight set well back. Inside the quality continues with a large elliptical hall and matching eye in the ceiling above. The stair is as slender as it can be, plain balusters, simple rounded handrail section – a fine Regency design *(see 76)*.

The historic gardens

The gardens of St Chad's are, historically speaking, some of the most interesting and complex in Durham. They lie above and below the castle wall, which in the college grounds has been largely rebuilt.

Above the castle wall, the gardens are as one would expect. Each Bailey property had its private rear garden, all ending at the castle wall or, by the eighteenth century, at railings and fencing *on top of* the wall, so owners could look out, to the riverbanks below – to Bow Banks – and a new opportunity for garden improvement.

What happened there is less easy to discover. The physical evidence is buried beneath vegetation, but the archives speak loudly. The 1:500 Town Maps of the 1st edition of the Ordnance Survey, dating from 1857 in Durham, are a wonderful and absorbing treasure, and on Bow Banks they record an unusual arrangement (**67**).

Documents suggest that Bow Banks once formed part of the medieval garden of the cathedral priory's infirmarer.[30] By 1806 they were being leased off in separate strips to the owners of the Bailey houses above.[31] But these narrow, steeply sloping gardens were not exclusively enjoyed. As the OS map reveals, diagonal and lateral paths cut across all the gardens, allowing neighbours to walk into each other's gardens. Unusually, it was a communal space of individual gardens, but an exclusive one, enjoyed only by those of a similar wealth and standing. Those, who Bailey residents might have put it, are 'people like us'.

The chapel and gardens

Those lower gardens are, for the time being, lost to us. The upper gardens still survive, now interlinked by a narrow path, and the journey

through them is a delight. Their great joy is that they are all of different character, and magically, from north to south, like Russian dolls, they get smaller. Let's take a walk.

Start in the great expanse of the lawn behind Francis Johnson's new buildings. A vast social space for college activities, framed on all sides, borrowing from Hatfield College and the riverbank trees. Admire Johnson's axial trick with

First edition of Ordnance Survey town map of Durham (1857), showing the communal gardens on the Bow Banks, below the present St Chad's College. (67)

Above: The chapel, St Chad's College. (68)

Right: Detail of the reredos in the chapel, St Chad's College. (69)

the cathedral and then move south to the chapel garden behind No 18.

Half hidden behind laurel hedges, the chapel might pass for a colonial mission church – small and utilitarian with freshly painted weatherboarding (**68**). You expect no more inside and certainly much is sparse and basic. But what strikes you on entering is the reredos. Fixed high on the east wall, of no great size, it is a gem. Erected in 1923 to a design by W H Wood, a Newcastle architect, it commemorates St Chad's fallen in the First World War. Richly carved, painted and gilded, it is all the more effective for its setting on a plain white wall (**69**).

Walk on south, through narrow openings in old burgage plot walls, drawn by the sunlight in the next garden *(see 187)*. It has a simple lawn and shrubberies where a seat and a table invite you to sit, but keep going, through an old brick wall, past a 'work-in-progress' space that could be another good outdoor room, to narrow No 21 with its fine rear gable. This garden is in two parts; the larger garden (near the house) leads onto a separate small compartment, cut off by a wall and hedge, enough for a single chair, ancient railings and little more (**70**). Journey's end.

Chad's gardens take you from the great to the small, from spaces that are sociable and communal to the solitary and contemplative. What unites them is the constant backdrop of the riverbank trees and the very effective use of just green shrubs and plants, in subtle shades, but no vivid colours. The result is very special.

No 5 THE COLLEGE

The college is leased from the Chapter and was once one of the canon's houses. Since 1981 it has been the home of first the Department of Palaeography and Diplomatic, now part of the University Library – a repository and public search room, holding some of the Library's most important archives (**71**).

It was one of the largest houses around the college green and behind its superficial Georgian exterior is a building with medieval fabric in the basement, altered at least twice after the Dissolution, then largely rebuilt *c*.1812. That was a time when external stucco or render was in fashion, and No 5 would have been covered in it. Now denuded for more than 30 years, in an age that venerates stone of any sort, it is time it had its coat back on.

Top: *'Smallest of all' – the garden behind 21 North Bailey, St Chad's College, with its post-1806 railings that once looked down on the new Bow Banks gardens.* (70)

Above: *No 5 The College.* (71)

STAIRCASES

The university has the largest collection of historic staircases in the city. They were, in their day, the epitome of fashion, and they serve as a barometer of centuries of changing style.

Medieval stairs were generally small, utilitarian, straight or spiral. Elizabethan stairs in Durham must have been little better, but none survive. Jacobean staircases are missing too.

The great popularity of staircases, as a statement of good taste, comes after Bishop Cosin's Black Stairs of 1662 in Durham Castle (*see 26*), the finest ever built in the city. Contemporaries built their staircases in oak, with a heavy high handrail and either bulbous or bine twist balusters (**72, 73**). Into the eighteenth century staircases were in painted pine, with lighter ramped handrails and thinner turned balusters; the side of the stair – the string – now openly decorated (**74, 75**). By the end of the century balusters were plain sticks and their mahogany handrails thin and sinuous (**76**).

Below left: *No 22A North Bailey (St Chad's) – a late seventeenth-century staircase with a high handrail and turned balusters, set on a pulvinated closed string.* (72)

Below right: *No 38 North Bailey – a late seventeenth-century stair with a broad handrail and bine twist balusters.* (73)

Left: *No 19(N) North Bailey (St Chad's) – a mid-eighteenth-century example with ramped handrail, turned balusters and an open string with curvilinear spandrils (ends).* (74)

Right: *D Stairs, (Hatfield), possibly c.1760 with a narrow handrail, thin balusters and continuous curvilinear spandil treatment.* (75)

Far right: *No 25 North Bailey (St Chad's) – an early nineteenth-century staircase with simple mahogany handrail and stick balusters, with an open string.* (76)

Eden House, St John's College, 3 South Bailey. (77)

ST JOHN'S COLLEGE

St John's College occupies the greater part of South Bailey. It was the home, in the eighteenth and nineteenth centuries, of many of the great county families, who kept their town houses here. St John's has the good fortune to own two of the best of them, belonging to the Edens and Bowes, the latter adjoining a once-magnificent riverbanks garden, the largest on the peninsula.

History

The college was founded in 1909, as St John's Hall, to enable prospective Church of England ordinands to receive a university education outside Oxford and Cambridge. It became a full college of the university in 1923, but remains independent of it, administratively and financially.[32] From its beginnings, non-theologians were admitted to the college, but numbers were initially small. In 1958 a separate hall within the college, Cranmer Hall, was formed as an Anglican theological college.

The college's first home was 6 South Bailey; No 4 was bought in 1910[33] and No 3 (Haughton House) followed in 1912 (77). By 1913 expansion had led to a new building – Cruddas House – built beyond the castle walls. Haughton House was extended *c.*1930, its rear garden landscaped in 1933/4.[34] The college gardens were at their best in this period, the Principal's Walk becoming something of a 'Durham showpiece'.[35] With further acquisitions, St John's stretched from 2–7 South Bailey,[36] later acquiring 28 North Bailey and 1 South Bailey. In 1987 the William Leech Hall was very neatly inserted into the college and its gardens

(HLB Architects). Off-site developments focused on the former St Margaret's Hospital, Crossgate, where the first accommodation opened in 1994, followed by the Crossgate Centre and Centre for Christian Communication.[37] In 1996 there was a major restoration of Haughton House[38] and in 2010–12 a new residential wing was added along with an elegant extension to the dining hall, both designed by Darbyshire Architects (**78**).

The Eden House

No 3 South Bailey (Haughton House) was once the Eden House, one of the most important houses in Durham. In 1721 the site was acquired by Sir John Eden with rebuilding probably following soon after.[39] Unusually, for the architecturally placid Bailey, this brand-new house had great presence, such that it is set high on a basement and set back so its impressive façade can be seen to best advantage.

Sir John's intention to be bold was not just skin deep; the house has innovations inside as well as out. Earlier Durham high-status staircases were often concealed from the entrance, rising through all floors to the roof. The Eden House followed the current fashion for presenting the staircase at the entrance, in a single great flight, to a first-floor landing (a secondary stair elsewhere took you higher) (**79**). The joinery displays great craftsmanship; each baluster has a finely carved fluted Doric column rising from an acanthus base. The carved spandrel ends of each step are expressed for the first time in Durham, turning a closed string into an open one. The handrail section follows current trends but is altogether much thinner, its sweep more elegant, anticipating the gradual reduction in its size through the rest of the century. Over time the other principal interiors of the Eden's house have been lost, but the best, the intended *tour de force*, survives magnificently.

At the back of his house Sir John reverted to cheaper brickwork and had only a modest garden above the castle wall. Given his obvious wish to impress, he might have wished to extend his gardening ambitions down the banks. That he didn't, suggests that he couldn't. And that was probably because, before 1728, his equally impressive neighbours, the Bowes family, had already secured all the land on the banks below his house for their own spot of aggrandisement, to which we must now turn.

The Bowes House

No 4 South Bailey, the Bowes House, is no match for the Eden's emphatic architectural statement next door. Its frontage is a long one, of three parts.[40] Firstly, from the north, is a small seventeenth-century cottage with a rear staircase projection, its street façade and much else rebuilt in 1862. Then a house, once two tenements on the north side of a common vennel, on the south

Dining hall extension, St John's College. (**78**)

side of which was the third part, another house originally perhaps three more medieval tenements. These houses were occupied during the sixteenth and early seventeenth centuries by a rich social mix of minor canons, professional advisors to the Chapter, cathedral workers and their families.[41] But by 1689 all of them were leased to Cuthbert Bowes. That date might be about right for the fine staircase in the second part of No 4, with fashionable bine twist balusters, but with a flat handrail, a feature of later seventeenth-century staircases in Durham (80). Its newel posts would originally have been adorned with ball finials above and pendant drops below – *de rigueur* for the fashionable stairs of the period.

About 1760, stylistically speaking, they renovated a large room, or rooms, just north of that fine staircase and turned it into a magnificent drawing room, now the Tristram Room (81). Newly restored in 1968,[42] when blocked west windows were opened up, the room is the best of its kind on the Bailey, though not in the city.

It is large but not grandiose. Some nice rococo plasterwork one would expect, good doorcases and window surrounds too, but what impresses is that all the joinery is finely carved, right down to the skirting boards. Two semicircular niches must have displayed some statuary or busts. Only the fireplace is a little later, added in a more restrained Adamish design. This, within their less than impressive, rambling pile of a Durham town house, was the Bowes' moment of opulence, meant to dazzle. And finally, as if to ensure that they were entirely in the fashion, the Bowes family doctored their old staircase, by removing the unfashionable finials and drops from their newels, and substituting flat caps... carved, of course.

If we leave the Bowes House, and head out to its garden, we need to briefly revisit the group of medieval tenements that stood here. One such was rebuilt around 1430 by John Lound, who rented land outside the castle wall, once the cathedral priory cellarer's orchard. In 1452 he acquired a

Above left: *Staircase, Eden House, 3 South Bailey, St John's College.* (79)

Above: *Staircase, Bowes House, 4 South Bailey, St John's College.* (80)

Left: *Tristram Room, Bowes House, 4 South Bailey, St John's College.* (81)

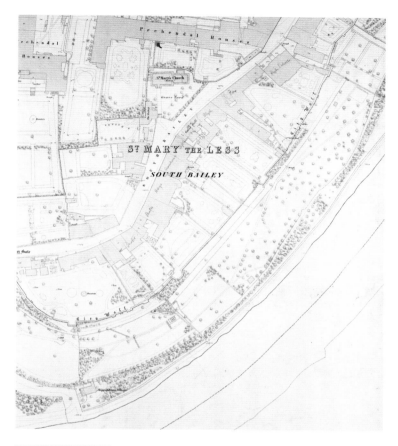

First edition of Ordnance Survey town map of Durham (1857), showing the great Bowes garden below the castle wall, now St John's College. (82)

The eighteenth-century Bowes family lived out most of their lives at their great Gibside estate, where another old rambling house sat within a vast, fashionably modern landscaped park. It is tempting to see a parallel here in Durham. Were the Bowes family prepared to suffer their relatively cramped living conditions provided they could lay out the greatest garden on the riverbanks, unlike their Eden neighbours of course, who manifestly had the house, but not the garden?

What they did was lay out a long terrace beneath the castle wall, incorporating the lower walls of a tower in the gardens of No 5. The medieval castle wall here is a major feature of St John's gardens and incorporates, from the south, a refaced half-octagonal tower, curious brick relieving arches of late date, then a largely medieval rectangular turret. Behind Cruddas House the wall has been rebuilt off old foundations to form a 'grotto', probably an ice house. Northwards is late twelfth-century masonry ending at the much-rebuilt large square tower.[43]

From the centre point of this terrace the Bowes family directed diagonal paths down the banks, joined by a path along the riverbanks (82). If the garden had been laid out early in the eighteenth century, the planting layout would have been formal, as is suggested by the radial and symmetrical paths. Later, and probably after 1816, they acquired an extra parcel of land beneath the tower of No 9. By the 1st edition OS map of 1857, the banks were informally planted with woodland trees. When St John's acquired the land they maintained the terrace, now renamed Principal's Walk. A short burst of activity in the 1990s saw the banks cleared and paths relaid, with new tree planting. While hopes of a large riverbanks

neighbour's small gateway made in the wall to gain access to his land. That gap in the castle wall remains the opening that the Bowes family used to gain access to their great garden and it still survives.

Without documents, the date of this great garden must be supposition. It may well have originated as the single plot of the medieval orchard spreading north and south along the banks, or it may have been land assembled over a period of time as the Bowes family gradually acquired their neighbours' lower gardens. Most probably it was in their control by the early eighteenth century, although the southern extremity of the garden is a later addition.

gardens restoration scheme await funding, much of the great Bowes garden is sadly returning to its natural state (**83**).

The remaining Bailey houses

The first house of St John's College is 28 North Bailey, a stone-fronted, late seventeenth-century house, with a heavily bolection-moulded doorcase. Inside is a contemporary staircase with a characteristic pulvinated closed string with dentil course, but a flat handrail, anticipating the handrails of the Georgian era.

No 1 South Bailey (Linton House) is a large seven-bay house of some pretension, probably dating from the early years of the eighteenth century. It was renovated in 1994.[44] The symmetry of its façade is disrupted only by a small door on the extreme northern end of the building. This lies on the boundary between the two Baileys and once gave access to a passage through the building that can be traced onwards right to the castle wall and down the riverbanks. Perhaps once the cathedral priory cellarer's path to his orchard, a right of way maintained long after the dissolution of the monastery? Inside, No 1 has a generous entrance hall, remodelled later in the eighteenth century, with stone and marble paving. This leads onto the original staircase, the broad one, still with a closed string and flat handrail, but no balusters, simply raised and fielded panels – the only staircase of its kind in the city. Outside, in the lower gardens of No 1, St John's students are, with great imagination, restoring the steep terraces to create an outdoor performance arena.

No 2 South Bailey is a narrow three-storey house that has fortunately yielded up some of its building history in recent years. During renovation work in the 1990s the front rendering was removed to reveal its stonework. This showed that the original house was a two-storey building of late seventeenth century date with very fine ashlar stonework, with bulls-eye closet windows flanking central mullioned and transomed windows (**84**).

The remaining Bailey houses of St John's had owners who could not match the wealth of the Edens and Bowes. Their houses, though fine, are consequently plainer and of less consequence. No 23 North Bailey is at least a seventeenth-century house, remodelled in later centuries. No 5 South Bailey is an eighteenth-century house with an early nineteenth-century staircase at the rear, flanked by rooms each with large semicircular bay windows. Its brick garden wall to No 6 is even earlier, probably late seventeenth century; 6 South Bailey (North) is a rebuilding of 1961 in a plain Georgian style.[45] No 6 South Bailey (South) is an early eighteenth-century house with pretty doorcase, and a slightly later staircase, with its bottom flight projecting into the hall, widened and swept at its foot. Finally, 7 South Bailey is of later eighteenth-century date, though its Greek doorcase with pediment and acroteria must have been built early the following century.

St Mary-the-Less

St Mary's has been used exclusively as the college chapel since 1919, before which it served as the parish church for South Bailey. Its public face proclaims its

Above: Principal's Walk, St John's College, formerly the Bowes garden. (83)

Below: No 2 North Bailey. A reconstruction as built c.1670 (top) and as heightened and remodelled in the late eighteenth century (bottom). (84)

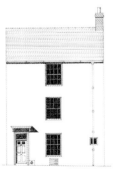

Above: Interior of the chapel of St John's College, formerly the parish church of St Mary-the-Less. (85)

Below: Garden view of 12 South Bailey, St Cuthbert's Society. (86)

1847 neo-Norman restoration (George Pickering, architect), but its rear walls are still largely medieval in date.[46] Architectural fragments, some rebuilt into the walls, attest its genuine Norman pedigree. Inside it contains a fine thirteenth-century stone relief from St Giles church, Durham, and a Cosin-period reredos. It was fully refurbished in 2002 (85).[47] At the church gate part of the old church rectory has been renovated by the college.

ST CUTHBERT'S SOCIETY

St Cuthbert's Society sits at the very end of South Bailey, occupying the tip of the peninsula within the castle walls. Its principal building is 12 South Bailey, evidently once a seventeenth-century house of singular quality. That quality still remains in part, as the college has the finest staircase of its date in Durham, after the castle's Black Stairs.

History and growth

St Cuthbert's Society was formed out of the crisis in the university's lack of growth in the 1860s. By 1870 the university proposed admitting unattached students, ie those who were not formally attached to a college. Male unattached students were first admitted in the following year and in 1888 they formed themselves into St Cuthbert's Society.[48] By 1893 it had a common room in Cosin's Hall on Palace Green[49] and a new boathouse followed a year later *(see 119)*.

In 1951 the Society was offered 12 South Bailey.[50] A year later it acquired 13 South Bailey opposite. In 1956 the main building was extended for more student rooms and two years later the dining room was extended (86).[51]

In 1962–3 the ground floor of 9 South Bailey was converted to the library, while plans for a new Junior Common Room between 12 South Bailey and the Watergate were also agreed.[52] In 1964 the new building was completed (Marshall Sisson, architect), at the same time as the Society took over 8 South Bailey. The then Principal commented in the annual report on the new building, noting that 'The Watergate extension … has been the subject of some adverse criticism, and one must admit that, if seen through the Watergate, it is not an inspiring building architecturally'.

The college houses

This short tour of the college houses briefly describes their historic interest, and culminates in its principal building, 12 South Bailey.

Nos 26 and 27 North Bailey are eighteenth-century buildings but the façade of No 26 disguises earlier fabric. Inside it has a staircase of two periods, early eighteenth century to the first floor, late seventeenth century above.

Nos 8 and 8A South Bailey originally formed a single house of *c.*1800. Inside the original staircase survives, a plain light handrail on simple square balusters, but praised by Francis Johnson as 'one of the most elegant staircases in the city ... its plan introduces a variety of charming serpentine shapes and spatial effects'.

No 9 South Bailey is a mid-eighteenth-century house containing a fine contemporary staircase with paired Tuscan columns instead of newels. Adjacent is a twentieth-century annexe, an Arts and Crafts conversion of the original stable. This was the home of the Shipperdson family at the beginning of the nineteenth century *(see 90–1).*

Across the road, 13 South Bailey is a later eighteenth-century house, with an early nineteenth-century staircase, plainly detailed but slender and elegant.

Finally, back across the road to 12 South Bailey, the college's principal building, in possession of a remarkable staircase and still something of a mystery (**87**). The building dates at least from the late seventeenth century, when its great well staircase was built, rising through three floors. In its scale and pretension it is bettered only in Durham by Bishop Cosin's Black Stairs in the castle. It has very large newel posts, strongly turned single bine twist balusters and a handrail so ostentatiously wide that a hand cannot grip it at all. This is the staircase as status, but a showpiece relying on scale rather than richness. Around the staircase hall are two contemporary doors in bolection-moulded architraves, with carvings of sheaves of corn and lion masks. With that promise, sadly little else follows. The building has lost its original interior, so we can never know whether that was as good as it got, or if there were other rooms as splendidly handled.

In 1900 the house was bought by John George Wilson who added the garden elevation and the impressive shell hood over the front door, and duly

Right: *Shell hood, 12 South Bailey, St Cuthbert's Society.* (88)

Below: *The castle wall path in the lower garden of St Cuthbert's Society, South Bailey.* (89)

Below right: *The Ice House, lower garden of St Cuthbert's Society, South Bailey, formerly part of the Shipperdsons' garden.* (90)

repeated the exercise at the entrance to his office at 5 North Bailey (88). He may also have commissioned the eighteenth-century-style plasterwork inside.

The college gardens and castle walls

The garden of 12 South Bailey fanned out from the back of the house, ending against the wide arc of the castle wall as it rounds the southern tip of the peninsula. The record of its layout on the 1857 1st ed OS map is very detailed – largely lawn with a central flower bed and adjacent fountain, flanked by three vases.

The castle wall here survives remarkably well. St Cuthbert's has one of the best and most original lengths of castle wall around the peninsula, albeit that some of its masonry is of rubble construction, rather than the usual coursed squared Norman stonework. A series of small towers and turrets, often refaced or rebuilt in their upper parts, are spaced along the wall, that behind 11 South Bailey linked to an eighteenth-century gazebo close by (89). They are familiar landmarks on eighteenth-century engravings of the peninsula.

Below the castle wall, the owners of No 12 could descend through the wall to another lawned enclosure below the western half of their Bailey garden. Below its eastern half was the garden of the Shipperdsons, a family living some distance away at No 9. They evidently wanted a riverbanks garden, but the great Bowes garden lay below their house, and so in 1816 Edward Shipperdson acquired the adjacent house, No 10, constructed a narrow path across its castle wall from his own house down into a riverbanks garden, beyond the Bowes garden. And there he built a Greek-style ice house (90), and

further down, on the river's edge, a garden room disguised as a small Greek Doric temple, where his family could take tea (**91**). His near neighbour, the architect Ignatius Bonomi may well have designed it. Known once as Shipperdson's Cottage, it is now better known, quite erroneously, as the Count's House, after the Polish dwarf Count Joseph Boruwlaski, who lived close by in the early 1800s.[53]

Top: *The Count's House, South Bailey, formerly part of the Shipperdsons' garden.* (91)

Right: *The treeless riverbanks, c.1700, with the Bishop's Barge, from a painting in the castle.* (92)

RIVERBANKS AND FULLING MILL

The river gorge around the walled peninsula served as a moat in the medieval period, and its banks remained treeless well into the eighteenth century. The medieval riverbanks were busy with corn mills, noisy and dusty with stone quarrying and a convenient repository for the effluent from the reredorters and garderobes of the peninsular buildings. In short, not what they are today.

The change began with the decline of quarrying during the sixteenth and seventeenth centuries, and the final expiration of the castle's

The Fulling Mill Archaeological Museum on the riverbanks. (93)

defensive role. By the end of the seventeenth century, Celia Fiennes noted that 'the walks are very pleasant by the riverside'. Both the Bishop's and Prebends' Walks – terraced gardens outside the medieval walls – had been built by then and the gardens below Hatfield College may well have been there too.

Sanitation improved, and by the mid-eighteenth century a number of southern panoramas of the city display the sweeping apron of the narrow-terraced riverbank Bailey gardens. Analysis of those engravings and paintings also highlights the gradual afforestation of the banks, but on the western side, below the castle and cathedral, this only appeared later in the century (**92**).

This 'natural' landscape was much appreciated at the time and when the new Prebends Bridge (1772–7) was sited away from the line of the old bridge, it was moved for a good reason. It offered the observer an unrivalled, and quite deliberately composed, panorama, as fine as any of the Romantic landscapes of Poussin or Claude. Above the Arcadian Fulling Mill shrouded in woodland and washed by the River Wear, rose the cathedral – the whole composition closed with a distant view of Framwellgate Bridge with open countryside beyond.

The Fulling Mill is not of course, merely a landscape sham but the best surviving of the medieval Durham's eight mills, one or two for each borough of the town. It was originally the cathedral priory's own mill, to which a second was later added *c*.1416 (**93**). These were known as Lead Mill and Jesus Mill, both now absorbed within the present Fulling Mill Archaeological Museum. The fabric is largely now seventeenth and eighteenth century, possible incorporating medieval work.

LEAZES ROAD

05

ST HILD AND ST BEDE COLLEGE

St Hild and St Bede College, with over 1300 students, is the largest undergraduate college in the university and also occupies the largest site – 6.7 hectares (16 acres) of sloping south-facing land bordering the River Wear, with spectacular views across to the cathedral and castle on the peninsula (**94**). Its origins lie in the separate foundations of two education colleges, Bede (for men) and Hild (for women) in the mid-nineteenth century.[1]

Both colleges initially specialised in teacher training, but in 1892 (Bede) and 1896 (Hild) became associated with the university, offering BA and BSc degrees alongside teacher training. The first three women graduates in 1898, were members of St Hild's College.

The two colleges were amalgamated in 1975 as the College of St Hild and St Bede, which subsequently became a University Council-controlled college in 1979. Each college was built in the Gothic style and both were extended considerably in the same manner during the rest of the nineteenth century. In the early twentieth century Bede College rebuilt its chapel and gave the city a building of hidden delights: an intriguing exterior worthy of passing comment, but within, an interior of great beauty. There was extensive work undertaken for the university's School of Education in the 1980s, and in 2003 a major repair and renovation took place throughout the college.

The peninsular panorama from the riverside at the foot of St Hild and St Bede College. (94)

The first buildings of Bede College. (95)

Bede College – main building

Early teacher training for men in Durham dates back to 1839. Two years later, the Durham Diocesan Training Institution opened at 103 Framwellgate.[2] In 1844 the Dean and Chapter gave the present site for the establishment of a college, work starting in 1846 and completed the following year, with accommodation for up to 20 students.[3] It was designed in a Tudor Gothic style by the architect George Pickering (the cathedral's Clerk of Works) assisted by George Mavin (**95**).[4] Many additions followed – a schoolroom in 1848, a practical room in 1850 and in 1857 the Principal's House was built. A year later the first Model School was added, and in 1875 further residential accommodation was added for 70 students. In 1884 a new Model School was built, the old one converted into the college chapel in 1886, when the training school became Bede College. Additions continued to be made to the college: science laboratories in 1890[5], and also, it is said, the largest gymnasium in the North of England.[6] Just before World War II work began on the new college chapel.

Bede chapel

The new chapel (1938–9, consecrated 1941) was designed by architects Seeley & Paget and was built to commemorate the centenary of the

Left: *The exterior of Bede chapel.* (96)

Opposite: *Bede chapel interior.* (97)

college.[7] It cost £11,000, then quoted as the cost of two Spitfires.[8] It is, architecturally speaking, the most important building in the college and one of the great, if too little-known, treasures of the whole university.

John Seeley and Paul Paget were important architects, whose practice flourished chiefly during the inter-war years and produced a number of highly original church buildings in a variety of styles. They are best remembered for their extension to the medieval Eltham Palace, designing a respectful Baroque exterior to disguise superb Art Deco interiors.[9]

Bede's is a plain rectangular chapel with a west tower-narthex and a low apsidal vestry on the south side. The exterior is extraordinary: the listing description whets one's appetite – 'art deco with gothic, baroque and classical detail' – and, yes, it's all there (**96**). But it works well, unified by a strong form and plain white rendered walls. The walls appear to be largely windowless until one discovers between the deep double buttresses framing each bay that narrow lancets sit in the buttresses' west walls. The tops of these buttresses, broadly Gothic in form, end, with a swept parapet, something of a Baroque flourish.

The interior is entered through the eighteenth-century doorcase from the college's first home in Framwellgate[10], and, at first, you anticipate more eclecticism within. What greets you is a single space of great intensity and tranquillity (**97**). An impressively plain white plastered interior, with each bay at ground-floor level lit by a narrow horizontal window, above which part of the side

walls move in towards each other on quadrant vaults. The rest of the walls stay on their line, rising to create recesses with light streaming in through those narrow west lancets. But entering from the west, the light source is invisible. It is a magical effect, one Sir Basil Spence replayed at Coventry cathedral two decades later. Higher up, the walls move still closer together to support a cross-vaulted ceiling – no ribs, just the thin junction of the vault webs, superbly lit from below. In contrast with this delicacy, the chapel stalls face each other with their fronts powerfully plain in alternate beech and walnut horizontal bands that carry the eye along to the east end, to the altar and the curtained reredos.[11]

The south front of St Hild College. (98)

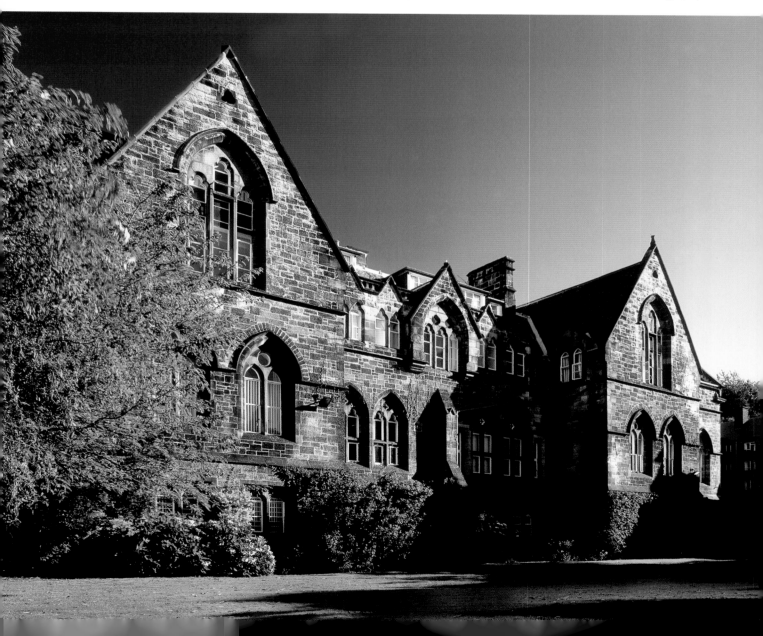

Belvedere House on Gilesgate bank. (99)

St Hild's College – main building

St Hild's College was built in 1858 to the designs of John Howison, County Surveyor, who also designed the old Winterton Hospital at Sedgefield. The original building has an H-plan core in a solid Early English Gothic style, but later additions were delivered in a lighter, but still Gothic, mood (98). The model school (1864) and new dining room and dormitory (1872) were both designed by a Mr Crozier. For the 1896 extension, including the first chapel and large schoolroom, W S Hicks of Charlewood & Hicks, was the architect. Further significant additions included a common room, laboratory and dormitory (1900), classrooms and lecture rooms in 1907, and in 1913 a new chapel was built. In 1923–7 more accommodation was provided by raising the roof an extra storey. All this twentieth-century work was designed by architects Joseph Potts & Sons. Still further additions were made after the war, but in a contemporary style.

The main college buildings at 'Hild and Bede' are an impressively large collection of institutional Victorian Gothic building, the style persisting into the twentieth century. Paradoxically, if sexual stereotyping is permitted, one cannot help but conclude that Bede, the men's college, has the more delicate light Gothic detailing while Hild has a far meatier and severe style. But what persists long in the memory is the moment of entry into the Bede chapel.

Belvedere, Gilesgate

Of the many buildings on the Hild and Bede site, only one more needs a mention. High on Gilesgate bank is the appropriately named Belvedere House, once a mid-eighteenth-century pair of dwellings, bigger than anything of its date around the green (99). What is intriguing is the use of the imposing Venetian sash windows, not for the main ground or first floor, but only up on the second floor, usually the domain of servants. Here, with the glorious prospect of the cathedral across to the west, the rooms have clearly been designed for family use. Best of all was the top western room, with a Venetian sash window in each of its three outside walls, an in-house belvedere enjoying a panorama with few equals in the city.

ELVET

SETTING

In the summer of 1956 the university was in trouble on the peninsula. It had been planning for more than five years to redevelop residential and departmental facilities in Owengate and North Bailey, development that involved the demolition of a number of important historic buildings. The scheme, designed by Thomas Worthington & Sons, later architects of Grey College, faced strong opposition from both Dr Thomas Sharp, the City Council's planning consultant and the City of Durham Preservation Society (forerunner of the City of Durham Trust). The university argued that new arts facilities were needed close to the peninsula. Matters dragged on into the winter with little sign of a satisfactory outcome.

New Elvet

Faced with this impasse, in late February 1957, the Warden of the university, Sir James Duff, wrote in confidence to Dr Sharp, whom he rightly identified as the scheme's most eminent and influential opponent. Sir James had reached the conclusion that though 'something pretty drastic will have to be done to the dilapidated parts of North Bailey and Owengate', he estimated even more development was needed and concluded that 'We must look elsewhere'.[1] He wondered,

what your reaction would be if we put forward a plan for buying up the buildings and ruins of buildings, between New Elvet and the river ... with a view to complete demolition and rebuilding for university purposes in a way that would, incidentally, give a decent frontage on the river ...

By the late 1950s this west side of New Elvet was an unhappy mix of traditional buildings, a sweets factory, a cleared site, a small council estate, a number of derelict properties and, to the south, a memorial garden (**100**). Thomas Sharp had said as much in his 1944 plan for Durham but had proposed the clearance of the whole of the west side of the street to allow a long unbroken

New Elvet, c.1909. By the 1950s most of the traditional buildings had been demolished. (100)

Dunelm House and Kingsgate Bridge. (101)

panorama of the east side of the peninsula. Such a proposal seems extraordinarily cavalier by today's conservation norms, but was not uncommon in a number of post-war historic town studies.

Sharp found Sir James' idea 'very appealing'. Though he cherished his great panorama, he knew it was unlikely to happen and thought that if development had to take place, university buildings would be best. He added that the new buildings 'should be broken so we can get views through them'.[2]

The Warden had only thought of acquiring land in the lower, northern half of New Elvet, but Dr Sharp pointed out the likely availability of land further south, much higher up near the Hallgarth Street/Church Street junction.

Sir James was delighted with Sharp's response, and he acted upon it; by the end of the year, the university was actively pursuing land acquisition there. Faced with the growth on three centres in Durham, the peninsula, South Road and Elvet, the university also began to give serious thought to how best to link them. As early as

1959 discussions were also taking place on a new footbridge between the peninsula and Elvet.

Old Elvet

The events that led to Sir James' letter, and the actions that followed, were perhaps not all prompted by the university's unhappy plans for the peninsula. As far back as 1944, Durham County Council had dreamt of leaving Shire Hall in Old Elvet and building a new County Hall at Aykley Heads. In 1956 these plans were still unrealised, but perhaps a confidential agreement had been reached with the council that the university would acquire their Old Elvet estate once they had finally built a new County Hall. If such an agreement existed in 1957, Sir James' letter never mentions it. In any event, on both counts – potential development sites in New Elvet and the probability of a major property sale in Old Elvet – an expansion east off the peninsula made good sense. The university had made its first tentative steps into Elvet.

KINGSGATE BRIDGE & DUNELM HOUSE

The story of Kingsgate Bridge and Dunelm House, for this is a story of the inseparable, begins with the university's decision in 1957 to expand east of the peninsula, first into New Elvet, later to acquire the County Council's Old Elvet estate.[3] A spine of new communal and departmental buildings was planned in New Elvet. At the head of the street was to be the Students' Union, almost the centre of gravity of the university estate, joined to the peninsular colleges and departments by a new footbridge across the gorge of the Wear. The result was two exceptional structures, elegantly described by Prof. Douglass Wise as 'the greatest contribution modern architecture has made to the enjoyment of an English medieval city' (**101**).[4]

Kingsgate Bridge

The university's commissioning of Ove Arup & Partners to design their new footbridge over the Wear was, with hindsight, an inspiration. It was a small commission by the standards of this international firm, led by the man who was already grappling with the enormous complexities of constructing the Sydney Opera House, working alongside architect Jørn Utzon. Ove Arup was quite entitled to delegate this small job to one of his team but, perhaps out of affection for his native North East (he was born in Newcastle), perhaps because he relished the challenge of such a sensitive site, he cherished this job as his own and devoted much time to it. It was his last personal design and he thought it his best.

The footbridge site linked Bow Lane on the peninsula with New Elvet, a desire line not lost on the citizens of medieval Durham, who also had, for a time, a Bow Bridge at this point. The site lay conveniently close to the planned new university developments, but at a point where the river was 36.5m (120ft) wide, with uneven bank tops 17.1m (56ft) and 20.1m (66ft) above the river, creating a valley 106.7m (350ft) wide at the top.[5]

At first it appeared that the limited finance available would only cover the cost of a short bridge, like its medieval predecessor, set at the bottom of the valley with steps and ramps up each side. But Arup experimented with various structural solutions based on reinforced concrete, and found that a pair of V-shaped supporting piers, each carrying one half of the walkway deck, was able to reduce spans and make a high-level structure, across the top of the valley, a reasonably cheap solution.[6]

Arup next examined the best line for the bridge. On the peninsular side, the point was fixed by the end of Bow Lane, but on the New Elvet bank, there were a number of options. Arup's first line ran square to the river, running further north than the final line and sloping 30ft along its length. Michael Powers, of Architects Co-Partnership, designers of Dunelm House, presented their first sketch scheme on this alignment in June 1961 with Arup, the Deputy County Planning Officer and the City Engineer in attendance. But the two council officers suggested an alternative, more southerly route for the bridge, to run diagonally across the river and keep the bridge deck horizontal, with only a short 3m (10ft) drop on the peninsular side. This line had the advantage of maximising the development potential on New Elvet, especially for Dunelm House. With hindsight it was also closest to the footpath route that ran south along Church Street, to the growing South Road colleges and science departments. The new line was agreed enthusiastically by Powers, who saw a better solution for his new building.

From the outset the cost of the bridge was critical. To avoid expensive scaffolding spanning the river, Arup designed an ingenious solution. His V-support piers and walkways would be built parallel to each other on opposite riverbanks, then rotated into their final position. The structure would be pivoted on temporary bearings built into the pier bases (**102**). Then three jacks, also built into the bases, described by Arup as 'rather like the screws on a surveyor's level', were adjusted to bring the bridge level. Where the two halves met, an expansion joint was needed that would prevent differential vertical movement, but allow free horizontal movement. After much experimentation the final interlocking bronze U- and T-shapes evolved as the best solution; though Arup added

Above: *Kingsgate Bridge under construction.* (102)

Right: *Kingsgate Bridge and the peninsula.* (103)

later that any notion that they stood for 'University' and 'Town' was purely coincidental.

Arup looked closely at the exit and entry points. The bridge foundation points on the riverbanks left a gap on the peninsular side, which had a wider and higher riverbank than on Elvet. A cantilevered abutment was constructed with steps rising up to Bow Lane. Its precise line was flexible and it gave the possibility of a change of direction at the junction between abutment and bridge. Arup himself wrote,

> *It was decided to make a change of direction at this point for several reasons; partly because by this means more trees could be preserved, partly because better views can be provided as one crosses the river, but mainly really because it just felt right to avoid the straight line.*

Aesthetically speaking, this change of direction, achieved at both ends of the bridge, is a masterstroke, responding with some humility to the surrounding trees and buildings. By creating

changing views, it cleverly delays the surprise of the main bridge deck, out over the river, until the last moment. Arup's own intuitive sense of good design is an altogether less arrogant solution than that unrelenting straight line (**103**).

The bridge's walkway was a generous 3m (10ft) wide, and externally it was articulated by a 2.4m (8ft) pre-cast module, accentuated by water spouts. Its solid walls were designed to offer some protection in inclement weather, with its parapet turning inwards to provide a wide support for leaning on to admire the views. Beneath this parapet there were originally fully recessed light fittings that gave an invisible light source when walking across the bridge at night. (These lights were later replaced with slightly protruding fittings following frequent vandalism).

Kingsgate Bridge was completed in 1963. To walk across it is to experience the drama of Durham's buildings and landscape, a thrilling journey that prompted Douglass Wise's opening remark. That journey was soon enriched by the construction of Dunelm House Students' Union alongside.

Dunelm House Students' Union

In May 1966, John Betjeman wrote to Vincent Harris, the architect of St Mary's College, to congratulate him on his design for Durham University's Students' Union building, exhibited at the Royal Academy that year. It was an unexecuted Palace Green scheme dating from 1944 (**104**).[7] Betjeman added that 'It … shows that the great architects, such as you … are still alive', a remark that must have been received by Harris with some poignancy, as the very same year the Students' Union had actually been completed, but not to his design.[8] Granted the site had changed, but by the 1960s his stylistic revivals were anathema to a

younger generation of architects, from whose ranks the Architects Co-Partnership were commissioned for the new Union in February 1961.

The building that arose in the heart of Durham during 1963–6 was, and remains, one of the most controversial twentieth-century buildings in the city. But perhaps the best. It was a building in the vanguard of the New Brutalism – a term unfortunately hijacked by those wishing to use it pejoratively to describe the harshness of some modern architecture of the 1960s and 70s, but in fact coined by Alison and Peter Smithson to describe the honest use of natural building materials, including Le Corbusier's favourite *in-situ* concrete – *beton brut*, probably the direct source of the name.

The Architects Co-Partnership design team was led by Michael Powers (partner-in-charge), although the building's designer was Richard Raine (job architect).[9] From the outset Ove Arup was part of the design team as consultant engineer,

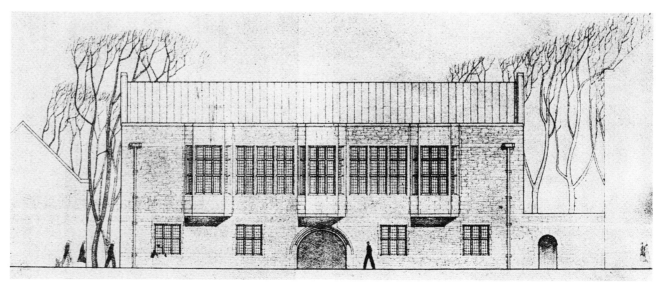

because of his deep knowledge of the site and his earlier authorship of the adjacent Kingsgate Bridge, from whose high-level walkway the new building would be very prominent (**105**).

The university's brief required substantial accommodation to be built on a steeply sloping site that stretched from the domestic character of New Elvet, down 15.4m (50ft) to the dramatic landscape of the Wear gorge where, right at the river's edge, the architects were to provide a boathouse. The site was cleared in late 1961, and at the end of the year outline planning consent was sought for both Kingsgate Bridge and Dunelm House on the newly agreed bridge alignment.[10] In February 1962 Powers presented their revised sketch scheme to

the university. Work began on site in 1963 and the building was completed in 1966.

Dunelm House operates on seven levels in all, its massing is small scale to the street, large scale to the river gorge, brilliantly reconciling the domestic with the heroic. Central to its design is the main staircase, which acts as a stepped spine, an internal street, running right down the building. It is immediately apparent on entering, an uninterrupted view from top to bottom that helps clarify the building's complex internal layout. In the original layout, bookshop, student newspaper and officers were on the top level, lounge bar and reading rooms down a level, then below them a café, coffee bar, sports rooms and kitchens. Still further down was a

Dunelm House from New Elvet. (106)

small hall at an intermediate level, and finally down again to the main hall at the bottom of the stairs, the largest space in the building cleverly dug deep into the riverbanks. Still further down, accessible from outside, was the boathouse.

These elements are articulated externally as a series of stacked boxes, lying back against the riverbank, their stepped profile reflecting rather than ignoring the natural topography. Looking out over the river, wide mullioned windows bring light deep into the building, the mullions, flush and unevenly spaced in some case, regular and projecting forward of the wall at other times, to model the wall surface.

All the structural walls, externally and internally, are built in that *leitmotiv* of the New Brutalism, *in-situ* concrete, shuttered in timber-moulds to impress the wood grain on the finished surface. The attention to detail and the self-imposed limitation on materials extend to the fine architectural detail too. The windows are visually frameless, set in metal against concrete mullions. Internally, the doors are hung from pivots to minimise framing, too. Small wonder that Arup as engineers were required to produce a stream of concrete detail drawings including ash trays and billiard table supports.

Concrete isn't limited to the walls. The roofs cascade in two directions and, from Kingsgate Bridge, arriving at the top of the building, they are very prominent and create, as often noted, a fifth elevation of the buildings, needing special care. The position of the footbridge deck here strongly influenced the design of the new building. Zinc roofing was originally intended as an economic material, before criticism from the Royal Fine Arts Commission led to a more expensive solution – specially designed interlocking concrete roofing slabs, giant tiles in effect – that reflect the traditional clay pantiles seen throughout the city.

The result is a building of dramatic sculptural form. The single-minded use of concrete for both walls and roof, giving the building a powerful unity (**106**). Its success is to take the most challenging of sites – topographically and contextually speaking

– on a steep river bank right before the east end of Durham cathedral and create an unflinchingly contemporary building that also displays great sensitivity to the Durham landscape.

ELVET RIVERSIDE 1 AND 2

The history of Elvet Riverside 1 is one of differing perceptions, of one client, five opinions, two architects and moving goalposts. Of how the designers of one of the city's most praised contemporary buildings went on to design one of its most unloved. It is, you should be warned, a story without a happy ending.[11]

As the Warden's 1957 letter to Thomas Sharp shows, the university perception was that the development of this site should be orientated towards the river. That emphasis may well have been in the mind of Marshall Sisson, architect

Professor Jack Napper's Masterplan for New Elvet, showing the four sites linked by a central student walkway. The northernmost site (right) was never developed. (107)

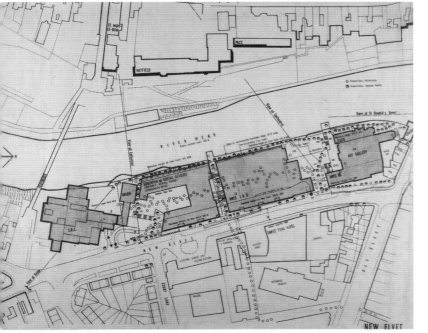

of the extensions to St Mary's College and St Cuthbert's Society, when in the summer of 1959, he was commissioned to design the first university building in New Elvet. His first design was opposed by Sharp, the revision accepted by him and the City Council, but then opposed by the County Council and the Royal Fine Arts Commission, the latter adding that it did not like Sisson's architectural treatment.

The scheme was revised, this time accepted by the County Planners with City Council approval likely. All seemed well. Then the County Council changed the site boundaries, setting back the building line to allow for a bus lay-by. Further revisions failed to impress the County Council and the plans were refused in April 1962. Three years on and no progress.

The university resolved to start again with a new masterplan by Professor Jack Napper, and new architects, Architects Co-Partnership (ACP), already successfully tackling the Students' Union at the top of the street.

Napper's masterplan showed four phases of development set apart to preserve cathedral views (**107**). Public access was to be extended to a cantilevered riverside walk, so elevations were important here. Students were to be directed up a central footpath spine through the whole site.

Despite the change of architect, in July 1962 perceptions were unchanged, when the university's Building Officer, noting the importance of Napper's riverside elevations, added that 'the City [Council] will be very interested in the site showing to New Elvet, which we ourselves will regard as the main vehicular access'.[12] It was clear that the university saw the street as the service entrance. ACP's first design, presented by Michael Powers, evidently

95

Elvet Riverside 1,
New Elvet. (108)

proposed a strongly monolithic elevation to New Elvet, worrying enough that the university was considering whether sculpture be added to relieve it. By the end of 1963 Powers 'confessed' that ACP were 'far from happy with the design' and proposed to table a much better solution.[13] The new scheme was poorly received by both councils' officers and Powers reluctantly recommended it be abandoned in January 1964 in favour of the earlier scheme.

Work started on site early 1965 and was completed the following year. The building was given its fully glazed 'front' elevation to the river, a central pedestrian spine and a rear wall to New Elvet unrelieved by any serious attempt at massing, modelling or architectural interest (108). Elvet Riverside 2 was built 1972–5, but Napper's central footpath was abandoned.

CHURCH STREET AND HALLGARTH STREET

The university estate includes two sites in Church Street, both part of Hatfield College. Next to Kingsgate Bridge stands a group of traditional eighteenth-century houses (Nos 31–33), while further along is James Barber House (formerly Palatine House), originally built as a County Council Hostel for the Blind. It has few architectural virtues but stands on the sites of an early coal mine and one of Durham's most extraordinary and short-lived buildings – a six-storey cotton mill that bordered St Oswald's churchyard. It was built in 1796 and destroyed by fire eight years later (109). Fragments remain in the wall and riverbanks.

In nearby Hallgarth Street, Hallgarth House (English Department) is the largest house in the street, outwardly eighteenth century but possibly

originating as part of the medieval manorial farm of Elvethall, many of whose buildings survive across the road.

OLD SHIRE HALL

When Durham County Council held its first elections in 1889, it had no home in the city. Having bought the Old Elvet site, it held an architectural competition for a new headquarters, won by local architects, H Barnes & F E Coates. The building was begun in 1896 and completed in two years, at a cost of £29,000 (**110**). Old Shire Hall, as it was later to be known, was the seat of expanding local government powers, and in 1905,

Above: *The 1796 Cotton Mill in Church Street, destroyed by fire in 1804, viewed from the south with colliery pithead gear in the foreground.* (109)

Right: *Old Shire Hall, Old Elvet.* (110)

only seven years after its opening, a new extension had to be constructed alongside. Between the wars, when further expansion was needed, the county council acquired the Georgian houses opposite and gradually populated much of the street with departmental offices.

This piecemeal expansion was no long-term solution and as early as 1944 the county council resolved to build new headquarters at Aykley Heads. Plans were produced soon after, but post-war austerity delayed a start, and it was only in 1963 that the new County Hall was finally completed.

The university, in this post-war period, was experiencing the same needs as the county council, expansion within a climate for austerity – hardly compatible bedfellows. Nevertheless, once the county council decided to move from Old Elvet, the university was equally determined to purchase the council's Old Elvet estate and move into their old buildings. It was purchased by the university in 1963 as their administrative centre, a role it fulfilled until late 2012 when that function moved to the Palatine Centre on Lower Mountjoy.

Old Shire Hall has a long symmetrical façade, faced in red glazed brick with plenty of terracotta detailing, a central dome above the main staircase hall and former committee rooms on each side. Internally the richness continues in hall, corridors and staircases finished in embossed and coloured faience. Behind this range is a hexagonal anteroom, panelled with Frosterley marble half-columns above, and beyond it lies the former council chamber, horseshoe plan at ground level, circular above with a dome on pendentives carried on more Frosterley marble shafts (**111**).

The building has a monumental scale quite at odds with the street, and that has led to an instructive debate about its merits – opinions on it changing dramatically over the decades. At the time of its construction the *Durham County Advertiser* loyally proclaimed that its design was 'exceptionally fine', but by 1937 Thomas Sharp condemned it as 'one of the most grotesque buildings ever erected in a city with any claim to architectural distinction'. In 1953, in an early exercise in precision bombing, Nikolaus Pevsner said that it was 'faced with that cursedly imperishable red Victorian brick, which is such crushing proof of technical proficiency and aesthetic dumbness'. Now, in the post-Betjeman era, awake to the delights of Victorian architecture, we forgive its arrogance, and delight instead in its rich warm tones, best seen from Elvet Bridge in evening sunlight.

Old Shire Hall interior. (111)

DOORCASES

Entrances are always the subject of improvement, so even in the city's small number of medieval houses, there are no doorcases of that age. The earliest surviving date from the later seventeenth century, the more vernacular examples still essentially late medieval in form – a chamfered surround and a shallow arched head (112). Higher-status buildings of that date had square-headed doorcases with moulded architraves, some with bulging bolection mouldings (113). By around 1700 all openings were squared, with architraves of varying richness, often topped by segmental, triangular or sometimes scrolled, pediments (114). These were usually 'broken' or 'open' in the Baroque period, but more classically correct by the middle of the eighteenth century, often incorporating semicircular fanlights and supported on flanking columns or pilasters (115). The thinner and more refined decoration of the late eighteenth and early nineteenth centuries are seen in several city doorcases (116).

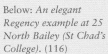

Below: *The late seventeenth-century doorcase (renewed) at the Music School, Palace Green.* (112)

Below: *A heavily bolection-moulded doorway, 28 North Bailey, St John's College, probably dating from the late seventeenth or early eighteenth century.* (113)

Above: *The c.1700 door surround at 45 North Bailey has been reset.* (114)

Below: *A mid-eighteenth-century doorcase in North Bailey.* (115)

Below: *An elegant Regency example at 25 North Bailey (St Chad's College).* (116)

OLD ELVET HISTORIC HOUSES

'Vanity of vanities, all is vanity!' The history of houses often comes down to this. We improve our houses not just for ourselves, but to impress others. And if we cannot rebuild anew, we can at least put on a good face and refront our ancient pile. The history of the university's Old Elvet houses, acquired along with Old Shire Hall, reflects this truth. In that they are similar to most of the houses that line the medieval streets of Durham.

After the Restoration in 1660, there was a period of marked renewal on the peninsula, catalysed by the figure of Bishop John Cosin, and the number of surviving staircases of the period, many in the Bailey colleges, attests to this.

This renewal may well have been evident in Old Elvet too, but the predominant characteristics of Old Elvet now point to a more substantial improvement in the eighteenth and early nineteenth centuries, but one that is often only skin deep. Complete rebuilding was rarely an option, more often new façades and perhaps a new staircase was added to an older building. A number of houses in the street have thick internal stone walls which are, no doubt, medieval or slightly later in date. The rear wing of 51 Old Elvet (Philosophy Department) may be entirely of that period, complete with its original roof.

Old Elvet was also in the eighteenth century a desirable address: the great Bowes family held a large house here – now the Royal County Hotel. Total rebuilding did occasionally happen – there is no finer group than 47–48 Old Elvet (Philosophy and English Departments), a tall early eighteenth-century range of great nobility and presence (**117**). If rebuilding could not be afforded, then refacing of the front elevation with new sash windows and

Nos 47–8 Old Elvet. (117)

pedimented doorcases was evidently fashionable, as at 42 Old Elvet (Applied Social Science and Sport Department). Internally, the staircase, once a concealed and unadorned flight, was given increasingly greater prominence, and many eighteenth-century stairs were introduced into Old Elvet at this time. The most *à la mode* are the mid-eighteenth-century *chinoiserie* examples, such as that at 14 Old Elvet (**118**).

The completion of the new County Court and Prison in 1820 led to a significant uplift in the surrounding property with some new buildings (eg 23 and 24 Old Elvet) and some with refurbished façades, as at No 29. Pressure for redevelopment led to the division of houses. Nos 44–45 Old Elvet originally formed one house, which were then divided in the early nineteenth century with pretty twin doorcases added. The *c.*1820–40 reordering of 30 Old Elvet is traditionally attributed the fine views of the public executions that could be obtained from its full-length first-floor balcony.

The Chinoiserie staircase at 14 Old Elvet. (118)

THE RACECOURSE

The Racecourse has been, for centuries, the recreational home for Durham citizens. Horseracing was held there, viewed from a stone grandstand. More recently it is better known as home of the annual Durham Miners' Gala. Special mention should be made of St Cuthbert's Boathouse (1894), an impressive building, as boathouses go in Durham, described at the time, with some verbosity, as 'not devoid of pretensions to architectural effect'.[14] Surprisingly accurate comments as it turned out: St Cuthbert's is the only college boathouse to become a listed building (**119**).

St Cuthbert's Boathouse, the Racecourse. (119)

MOUNTJOY AND MAIDEN CASTLE

LOWER MOUNTJOY – SETTING

The first buildings of the new Science Laboratories appeared in 1924, on an old colliery site at the junction of South Road and Stockton Road. Since then, in nearly a century of growth, the site has become almost fully built over. It was a growth, once planned but increasingly, as time went on, *ad hoc* and taking little account of the aspirations of early architects and planners. Open spaces, elsewhere in Durham manifestly as important as the buildings that enclose them, were seen at the 'Science Labs' as opportunities only for being built on. It was fair to say in the early 1990s that, with some notable exceptions, architecturally and spatially speaking, the site was a disappointment, responding to the demands of teaching and research with little thought for wider environmental considerations.

The aspiration to do something better with the site was always in the mind of the university, and in recent years the building of the Calman Centre and its landscaped apron gave Lower Mountjoy, as it is now known, a focal point for the first time. Since then the university has built on these strengths with buildings of quality, some not without their highly controversial aspects. What they then did was pull this disparate collection of buildings together into a comprehensive

Sir William Whitfield's Science Library, Lower Mountjoy. (120)

landscaping scheme that banished cars and laid out generous pedestrian paths throughout the site. The result, seen from within, is a remarkable and successful transformation.

LOWER MOUNTJOY – A PERAMBULATION

The walk through the site starts in the NW corner, at the New Inn junction, and proceeds westward. *En route* the main eight blocks of development are described – Library, Geography, Dawson Building, Physics, Calman Centre, Chemistry and Maths, Engineering and finally the new Palatine Centre and Law School.

Right: *The north elevation of the 'West Building', Lower Mountjoy.* (121)

Below right: *Institute of Hazard and Risk Research, Lower Mountjoy.* (122)

William Whitfield's Science Library of 1963–5 still anchors the corner of the site with a boldly simple building, executed in his favourite brown brick for the solid shafts that conceal the stacks, alternating with full-height narrow lights to the carrels (**120**). The building was sympathetically extended south and west in 1982–3 (Faulkner Brown, Hendy, Watkinson & Stonor). A further addition was made in 2012 *(see Palatine Centre)*, when it was renamed the Bill Bryson Library.

The design of the Geography Department building of 1950–2, (originally the 'West Building' for Geography and Maths), is credited to Professor J S Allen, author of the 1947 University Plan. It was seen as the first instalment of its implementation and rightly set a high standard (**121**). Against the traditionalist architecture of Durham colleges – St Mary's was under construction across the road at the same time – this was a thoroughly contemporary building, in the emerging Festival of Britain style. In fact the building was designed by the young William Whitfield, Allen's assistant at the time. The brief called for multi-departmental uses to be accommodated along with a large lecture theatre and library, each element individually expressed in a dignified and balanced composition, using a variety of materials: brick, stone and copper roofing. The interiors are equally impressive.

Into the building's southern front, once viewed as its principal façade, a newcomer has crept in. Unlike earlier infillings, the Institute of Hazard and Risk Research (2007–8, Atkins), is rather a good one – low, respecting its grander neighbour, well-articulated and clad in glass and warm red sandstone (**122**).

The Dawson Building was, in 1924, the first Science Laboratory on the site – single storey in plain brick. Richer façades were planned in 1937 when it was proposed to double the height, and reface three sides *(see 13)*; in the event wartime construction (1939–40 Marshall, Tweedy & Bourn) understandably put the dampers on things. The building was extended again in 1974 (Cusdin, Burden & Howitt) and refurbished in 1996.

The Library, Dawson and Geography buildings enclose one of the new communal spaces in Lower Mountjoy. It was, as a space, potentially always there, but compromised by cars, hedges and fragmentation, just waiting for the better definition and materials the new landscaping introduced (2012, Space, Nancy Corbett, landscape architect).

Behind Geography lies the sprawling Physics buildings, starting with the main ranges to the north, in parallel with Geography. Begun in 1958 (Woodside), the main range followed to the west and south by 1962 (Easton, Robertson, Cusdin, Preston & Smith). Four extensions followed (1967–95). In 2002 the Ogden Centre was added with its acutely angled glazed entrance (Nicholson Nairn).

Moving west leads to the Calman Learning Centre and EGG building, completed in 2007 (Building Design Partnership), the former a diversely panelled rotunda clad in shades of grey sheeting offset with green and blue randomly set glazing (**123**). The centrality of the building form and its rather dazzling exterior does just the right job in creating a sense of arrival in the heart of Lower Mountjoy, all reinforced by generous landscaping.

Across the road to the north is the largest building group at Mountjoy: the Chemistry and Maths block. It has grown considerably from its origins as the Chemistry Building Phase 1 (Cusdin,

Burden & Howitt). The much larger second phase was designed by the same architects in 1962–4. During the following decades extensions along, behind and on top, continued to fill up the surrounding area, perhaps only Dewjoc's cleverly articulated Chemistry extension of the late 1990s and the Material Chemistry block raising standards.

Opposite, on rising ground in front of woodland, the Engineering Science Department was established in 1963–6 (Cusdin, Burden & Howitt). Like Chemistry and Maths, it is another

Above: *The Calman Learning Centre, Lower Mountjoy.* (123)

Below left: *The School of Engineering and Applied Sciences.* (124)

large building of varying shapes and materials, that fails to match the quality of the West Building. It was only in 1986–8 that excitement returned when Faulkner Brown, Hendy, Watkinson & Stonor, in their School of Engineering and Applied Science, very successfully articulated two long glazed tile and glass buildings either side of a glass atrium.

Bringing back the woodland to wrap itself around the buildings creates a very attractive interplay of the natural and manmade (**124**).

Finally onto Lower Mountjoy comes the new Palatine Centre, Law School and Library extensions, bordering Stockton Road, opened in 2012 and designed by PH Partnership, with Space. This flagship university building has a striking elevation to the road, of alternate curved glazed bays, one receding and then one thrusting out high into the sky, visually, but not structurally, supported on similarly curved laminated-timber legs (**125**) The plasticity of this design, decidedly insect-like in form, continues at its eastern entrance (Law School), beyond which there is a central glazed atrium running the length of the building to the western end (Palatine Centre). Further west is the extension to the library (recently renamed the Bill Bryson Library), more conventionally expressed in a deep glazed arc (**126**). Inside, a large art collection is on display, including works by John Tunnard, Fay Pomerance, Sandra Blow, Victor Vaserely, Alexander Calder, Terry Frost, Andy Warhol, Fenwick Lawson, Victor Pasmore and Henry Moore.

Above: *The Palatine Centre on Stockton Road, Lower Mountjoy.* (125)

Right: *The Bill Bryson Library, Lower Mountjoy.* (126)

UPPER MOUNTJOY

Behind the uppermost trees of Little High Wood, on the city's sensitive skyline, always a backdrop to the cathedral, the university has gradually been able to develop, subject to strict planning limitations on height. This constraint has fortunately not limited creativity, as William Whitfield's strongly modelled Psychology Building (1966–70) demonstrates, with military allusions in its battered walls, rows of mullioned windows and bold towers (**127**). Later buildings, similarly in the lee of the hill when seen from the city centre, include the large Biological Sciences block (1992–4 Dewjoc) and the triple-armed Mountjoy Research Centre (now Mountjoy 1, 2 and 3) of 1983–5 (Hawkins Heath Partnership), extensively remodelled internally in 2011 (GSS Architecture).

Above: *Psychology Department, Upper Mountjoy.* (127)

MAIDEN CASTLE

The wooded Iron Age hill fort at Maiden Castle is still one of the most powerful features in the natural landscape of the River Wear as it approaches the Durham gorge. Set high above the river's flood plain, it has given its name to the sports fields and buildings that have been established there, off the east side of the Shincliffe Road. The first sports hall dates from 1962–5 by Cordingley &

Below: Maiden Castle Sports Centre with the Iron Age hill fort beyond. (128)

Right: Ove Arup's bridge at Maiden Castle. (129)

McIntyre, extended in 1997 by Waring & Netts, and again in 2011 by the same architects, now Space (**128**).

To the east linking the main site with further sports fields across the river, is Ove Arup & Partners' cable-stayed footbridge of 1974, its deck elegantly slung from raking supports set on one bank (**129**).

SOUTH ROAD: WEST

08

SETTING

South Road rises out of the city from the head of Church Street, running almost straight towards Farewell Hall and the old Great North Road, and along its length in the early nineteenth century a number of villas and country seats were built, set in generous gardens and parkland. The university inherited farm estates here from the Dean and Chapter, and gradually consolidated its land holding as successive development plans identified the area for university expansion.

The first new colleges, built after World War II, were able to take advantage of their open sites – fields gently sloping to the north – to gain a peninsular view. Later colleges, set on the flatter or southern-facing higher ground, in open fields, parkland or woodland, lost that panorama and made their own landscapes (**130**). The last college to be built, far removed from cathedral views, ingeniously reclaimed that prospect.

ST MARY'S COLLEGE

St Mary's College was the first complete new college building built by Durham University. It was also the first to be sited off the peninsula, but laid out to maintain a strong visual link to it. Vincent Harris's design, of long gestation, though traditional in form, has inventive and powerful massing. Some of

its external spaces are amongst the most beautiful of all those in the university campus.

History

The first hostel for women students opened in 1899 at 33 Claypath, two years later moving to Abbey House on Palace Green; in 1919, now with collegiate status, it moved again to 8 The College.[1] Additional houses were leased as the college grew still further, and by 1934 the university had agreed new college buildings were needed on the site at

A late 1960s view of the western colleges on South Road, with St Aidan's (left) and Van Mildert (right), with Trevelyan and St Mary's colleges behind the latter. (130)

108

St Mary's College — Durham

Charley's Fields.[2] Early in 1935 Vincent Harris was invited to become the architect.[3] Harris's career up to then had been predominantly focused on his civic buildings, such as Sheffield City Hall,

Manchester Central Library and Leeds City Hall, although since 1930 he had also designed at Exeter University.[4] By 1936 Harris had produced his first plans for St Mary's, for a college of 60 students (**131**). With the outbreak of World War II in 1939, all hope for the new building faded.

After the war, the college and Harris returned to their plans, but they were extensively modified by increased student numbers; first 80, then 100 and finally 120 students were to be accommodated.[5] Eventually, in October 1947, work began on site.[6] The college was part occupied in 1951 and fully occupied by 114 students the following year (**132**).[7]

The college has a main communal block of two storeys with basement, flanked by residential wings of three storeys with attic and basement.[8] To the west is a long wing housing the dining hall with its own ceremonial entrance and, beyond it, the kitchen courtyard. As the University Grants Committee would not fund the proposed new chapel, and as his student numbers increased, Harris repositioned it as a new NE residential wing, still linked by a cloister, but now swung through 90 degrees, so that its west façade closed the main approach to the college. The whole building is clad in Otterburn stone with steeply tiled roofs (**133**). Devoid of new furnishings, the college approached Robert Thompson of Kilburn (the 'mouse man') to provide a High Table, 20 chairs, Principal's chair and sideboard for the dining hall.

Vincent Harris might have been allowed a little time to reflect on a job well done, but in March 1954 he was again approached by the college to increase numbers up to 150 students. Harris was not enthusiastic about inserting more windows into his elevations, but a compromise was finally reached and alterations put into effect. In the same year the lime avenues were planted along the main drive.[9]

When pressure to increase student bedrooms arose again, in 1959, Marshall Sisson was asked to design the new buildings, away from the main college, down the slope to the north, still respecting, with a slight variation, Harris's site axis. Completed in 1962, the new buildings were two three-storey wings and a lower linking two-storey block, so designed that the view to the cathedral should not to be obscured as 'the citizens of Durham still had the right to walk across the forecourt to admire the view'.[10]

Left: *Dining hall entrance, St Mary's College.* (133)

Above: *George Pace's chapel interior, St Mary's College.* (134)

Two years later, the dining hall was enlarged by inclusion of the corridor and anteroom. Four new staff houses were also built, to the designs of (now Sir) William Whitfield. In 1970, in the roof of the NE wing, the cathedral architect, George Pace, ingeniously converted the roof space to a chapel of dark Nordic character (134).[11] William Whitfield's plans for an enlarged dining hall and 80 extra student rooms, set out in his University Development Plan 1971–80, came to nothing.[12]

In 1991 the university's Estates and Buildings Department (J G Butcher) designed the extension to Sisson's 1962 block to provide 79 extra bedrooms. Conference facilities were completed in the same year. St Mary's College also occupies Elvet Garth, a small Victorian villa close to South Road, with fine first-floor stone bay windows on its north front.

Appreciation

The year of St Mary's completion, 1952, was a year after the Festival of Britain on the South Bank in London, a showpiece for all that was contemporary in modern architecture. St Mary's College might have seemed a building out of its time. However, despite the rapidly changing social context in which St Mary's was built, the forces of modernism in architecture were only to dominate from the middle years of the decade. It was, of course, like so many post-war buildings, a design that had evolved over two decades and in its architect, Vincent Harris, the university had appointed an unrepentant traditionalist. What is beyond doubt is that it was greatly admired in its day, and no wonder. In the generosity of its layout, the inventiveness of its detailed design, and the beauty of its grounds, St Mary's is a very fine building indeed (135).

The approach, from the west along the lime avenue, cuts right in front of the building, its axis closed by the embellished doorway of Harris's NE wing. The kitchen court has an appropriately modest Vernacular Revival feel, with high stacks and an arched gateway with Lutyens doors. Beyond are the stone steps and columns of the dining hall portico, by far the grandest entry into the college, sadly now unused but still fine theatre.

Further east is the main entrance, fronted by a forecourt edged in stone (restored 2012). Above a flight of steps, set on the great axis that fixes the whole geometry of the college, is a surprisingly simple doorway. Harris's intention was, perhaps, not to place the emphasis at the centre of his composition, but out on the flanks that frame it, on the taller residential wings, and here is some of the boldest work in the college. The need for tall flues from the boilers in the basement of the west wing would have upset the symmetry of the façade, and Harris solved that problem by replicating the boiler room's huge stone stack three times over, to create dummy stacks that both articulate the main façade and ingeniously help frame the doorways into the southern court,

Once within the central block, the interior of the college continues the essentially English Baroque themes of the exterior, with a delicately coved ceiling to the main dining hall, and black-and-white tiled floors in the corridors. The staircases are especially fine, with shapely turned balusters rising around an open well through the floors (**136**).

Harris's classicism was very broadly expressed. It could be respectfully copyist, as in the dining room portico, or inventively baroque, as in the residential block doorways. It could also be strikingly original, almost contemporary, best seen in his powerfully simple cloister arcade that links the main college to the added NE wing (**137**).

Moving into the large southern court, the space is framed on three sides by buildings, the central block modelled with full-height bays. The taller residential wings are entered through Harris's

Left: *The dining hall, St Mary's College.* (136)

Below: *The cloisters, St Mary's College.* (137)

Above: *Statuary on the south lawn, St Mary's College.* (138)

Above right: *Zen garden, Lafcadio Hearn Centre.* (139)

most emphatic and original entrance doorways, set beside the great 'stacks' (1). This court was originally intended, in early designs, to be closed by a cloister walk, but as so often happens in Durham colleges, the landscape closes the space instead. In place of a cloister walk, Harris chose to embrace a wider landscape, not squaring and closing the space, but arcing his beautiful stone-paved footpath out in a great semicircle towards a grove of mature trees (**138**).

His landscaping advice was actually to allow flowers in areas south of the college, but although that may have suited an enclosed courtyard, once he closed his court with trees, such fussy planting would have been wrong.[13] So, thankfully, his advice has been ignored in the past 60 years. Here it should remain as it is, nothing but the greenery of shrubs, hedges and trees, nicely enhanced by the careful siting of a little classical statuary under the branches. It is a perfect space. Don't touch it.

TEIKYO UNIVERSITY BUILDINGS

The 'Teikyo University of Japan in Durham', was established at the university in 1990 to provide facilities for the students in their year spent in Durham. The first buildings to be completed in 1989 were the Shoichi and Etsuko Halls of Residence, both close to St Mary's College and taking their traditional theme from the NE wing of Vincent Harris's design, but executed in brick instead of stone.[14]

The Lafcadio Hearn Cultural Centre, opened in 1990 (Shepherd Design Group on behalf of Shimizu UK Ltd) is sited close to the Oriental Museum, and has a far more contemporary feel. If there is no hint of Japanese influence on the exterior, all changes on entering the inner court. The offices and teaching rooms are white-walled, lit by windows with strongly horizontal glazing panes, and set around a beautiful Zen garden (**139**).

TREVELYAN COLLEGE

Trevelyan College is well known as the 'hexagonal' college, a composition of interlocking polygons, large and small. It is also known for its highly successful integration of buildings and landscape, a significant

Trevelyan College in its grounds. (140)

achievement given that, unlike other South Road colleges, it inherited little or no mature vegetation. While much of the college has an introverted warmth about it, its dining hall has a more imposing ambition, perhaps the most successful space in the university where contemporary art and architecture work so well together.

Origins and development

Trevelyan owes its conception to the UK government's drive in the early 1960s to expand university education. The year 1963 was to be the start date, and, in anticipation of this, in 1960 the University Grants Committee (UGC) asked all universities to prepare their development plans for accommodating more students. Durham's response to the UGC was to propose three new colleges on land it owned south of the river. There

were to be two men's colleges, 'X' (later Van Mildert, 350 men) and 'Y' (later Collingwood, 350 men), to open in 1963 and 1965 respectively, and a women's college, 'Z', to open in 1966.[15]

College 'Z' (later Trevelyan College) was to be built on farmland, part of the Elvet Hill estate. The site was largely devoid of trees with just a small stone potato store on the side of Elvet Hill Road.

In March 1963 the outline proposals for the site included not only a new college, but also a 1500-seat assembly hall as well. The County Planning Office thought the site too small for both and set development constraints that would protect views from Elvet Hill.[16]

In July 1963, from a shortlist of two, Stillman & Eastwick-Field, a London architectural practice, were appointed, with partner John Eastwick-Field (partner-in-charge) and Humphrey Lukyn

Williams (job architect).[17] Later, Brian Hackett was appointed as the landscape consultant.

The brief for the college was confirmed in August 1963 and design work began with early sketch schemes for bedroom layouts, yet to adopt the hexagonal theme.[18] By March 1964, site layouts were adopting that plan form, the University Building Committee noting without opinion that 'the study bedrooms were of irregular shapes' (**140**).

Further uncertainty about the overall college layout arose in June, when the architect was made aware for the first time of the Whitfield Plan, a university-commissioned report by fellow architect William Whitfield into traffic and car parking issues in South Road. A planned new road had to be accommodated, and as a consequence the college moved northwards on its site.[19] Further complications arose when poor ground conditions, including mine workings below,[20] required

adjustments to both plan and structure; the whole college was built on a concrete raft foundation, supported on 260 piles.[21] Building began in 1965 and it was completed in 1967; students moved in later that year, in September.

The college plan was a series of interconnecting hexagons, set around courtyards, thus avoiding the need for long corridors. The hexagonal spaces also enabled greater accessibility to adjacent hexagonal spaces than would be possible with a conventional orthogonal plan. This all assisted in improving college security, an important consideration in what was planned to be a wholly women's college.[22] The shorter corridors gave access to the study bedrooms in units of six round a landing and kitchen.

The college site included very few mature trees and Hackett's landscape plan, approved March 1967, was duly implemented with extensive tree and shrub planting. Within the building complex a new birch tree was planted in the main courtyard. Eastwick-Field was particularly keen that the existing and new trees acted as a foil for large areas of brickwork, and he also encouraged the use of traditional estate fencing along the southern boundary of the college (**141**)

Trevelyan was an undecorated building, internally of plain brick or blockwork, none plainer than the vast empty walls of the dining hall – a vastness that required an artistic response that emphasised the great scale of the space, rather than one that sought to mollify or lessen it. In May 1968, the college's new Art Committee set aside money for a single art work, after which John Walker, an abstract painter, was suggested by the Arts Council as a suitable artist.[23] Examples of his work were hung in the hall and in 1971 he was commissioned

The old beech at Trevelyan College. (141)

*The dining hall,
Trevelyan College.*
(142)

Above: *K Block, Trevelyan College.* (143)

Below right: *Trevelyan's rich parkland landscape.* (144)

to produce three paintings (**142**). Two years later, Walker was proposing to produce five paintings,[24] and he later gifted a sixth.[25] The resulting fusion of art and architecture is a great success.

In 1969 the university's plans for expansion envisaged the construction of the long-planned large hall as well as 50 extra bedrooms at the college. In the event, only the hall proceeded, Eastwick-Field again being asked to produce a design.[26] By 1971 the new road proposed by William Whitfield had been abandoned and on its site arose the Sir James Knott Hall (1972–3).

The new college did not sweep all before it. There were a few trees saved and, with commendable forethought by university, college and architect, the small stone potato store on the boundaries of its site was also kept. It served both as a visual foil to the new buildings behind, but more importantly it was a reminder of past land use, the simplest expression of that vital and enriching resource for all landscapes – 'time depth'. In 1978, it was restored and was dedicated the following year as a place of Christian worship. The chapel now also accommodates other appropriate uses.[27]

The later twentieth-century expansion of all the university's South Road colleges threatened to upset the delicate relationship between buildings and landscape that the original designers had sought to establish. That equilibrium was never more at risk than at Trevelyan, where the initial relationship had been so beautifully balanced. Fortunately the enclosure of the cloisters (1979–80), library extension (1982–3) and later 50–bed K Block (1989–91), all designed by architect, Dennis Jones, were very successfully assimilated (**143**).

Appreciation

The London architectural practice of Stillman & Eastwick-Field established a reputation in the post-war period for producing contemporary architecture of a high standard. John Eastwick-Field's designs for Trevelyan reveal an almost obsessive tenacity in developing the hexagonal theme, cleverly used for two different effects – in most of the college, regular, small and intimate, and in the dining hall, irregular, large and monumental. By limiting the architectural forms and by keeping to a small palette of consistently used building materials and details – unusually, windows are set back in their reveals a full brick length – his design achieves a powerful unity (**144**).

of South Road and Elvet Hill Road. Once a public house called The Shepherd's Inn, it was bought by the Fogg-Elliotts of Elvet Hill in the mid-nineteenth century, its stables converted to cottages, and the whole property let as dwellings (**145**). Thick internal walls suggest an older building may survive beneath the extensive early nineteenth-century remodelling.[29]

Left: *Southend House, South Road.* (145)

Below: *Van Mildert College.* (146)

Within the college, there is a delightful intimacy generated in its smaller spaces, its maze of short corridors and student rooms, spaces humanised with small-scale paintings and prints, many by Julian Trevelyan and Mary Fadden. Those corridors are so narrow you have to acknowledge passers-by – the design prompts human contact. Bedrooms are commendably private, but in some central offices, you are overlooked – your conduct can be monitored. This is the realm of 'architectural determinism', the creed much espoused in the 1960s and 70s, that building design can strongly influence social behaviour. Susan Martin, author of the college history, has spoken at length of the varying ways in which the building design influences how students and staff use the building and relate to one another.[28] Perhaps more in Trevelyan than any other Durham college this thesis may have some truth.

SOUTHEND

Southend, now the School of Government and International Affairs, is an attractive group of traditional buildings standing right on the corner

VAN MILDERT COLLEGE

Van Mildert is 'the college with the lake'. It is also the most public of the university's post-war colleges and here, in an age of hard-nosed modernism, architect Philip Middleton created a romantic landscape that is held in great affection by the countless travellers who pass by on South Road, on their way into Durham (**146**).

The college was named after William Van Mildert, the bishop of Durham who was instrumental in the university's foundation in 1832. It was one of the three new colleges proposed by the university in 1960. The university had hoped to hold an architectural competition for the new college, but this was resisted by the national funding body, the University Grants Committee. Consequently, in February 1961, the university appointed Phillip Middleton of Middleton, Fletcher & Partners of Middlesbrough as architect for the new college.[30] At that time he was overseeing the completion of his new Gulbenkian Museum of Oriental Art building (now the Oriental Museum) at Elvet Hill, and his appointment, no doubt, reflected not just professional competence and good design skills, but also some familiarity with the chosen site which lay adjacent to the new museum – adjacent and, to be precise, below. It may well have been apparent to Phillip Middleton during his many museum site visits how waterlogged and flooded were the fields on the corner of South Road and Elvet Hill Road.

The college building began on site in 1962 and it was completed in 1965. The college was extended to the SW by the addition of Middleton Stairs (1972) and the Conference Centre (1986). The college later expanded in two phases towards Elvet Hill Road, an expansion that never threatened the original concept of the college.

The sites of all three new '1960s' colleges were effectively self-contained and introverted. They stood on ground with trees to the north, unable to include, as a determinant in their site layout, some distant panorama of the cathedral, as Grey and St Mary's colleges were able to do. In landscape terms,

Bay windows at Van Mildert College. (147)

Van Mildert, Trevelyan and Collingwood had to make do with what they had on site. Collingwood had big trees, but Trevelyan had to plant most of theirs. And as Middleton soon realised, what the Van Mildert site had was an abundance of water, draining into it from the surrounding higher ground. In his first sketch scheme, presented in February 1962, Middleton found Van Mildert's *genius loci* as a 'place of water', created a lake and developed his college layout around it.[31]

The composition of original college buildings is formal and impressive with four four-storey ranges of conventionally corridored, study bedrooms, three to the SW around a grass court, then the great dining hall block and the fourth range to the NE, set around the lake. Each block is faced in buff brickwork with an inclined pairings – like butterfly wings – of full-height triangular bay windows (**147**). The dining hall block continues the butterfly wing theme that models the façades, but here with a much more monumental scale, setting the tall narrow windows between full-height and canted concrete fins that rise above the roof line to form a serrated silhouette. Around the lakeside, all ground floor plans are cut back to accommodate a covered cloister walk.

The college is entered from much higher ground to the NW of the site, off Millhill Lane.

Above: *The dining hall, Van Mildert College.* (148)

Below: *Van Mildert College.* (149)

the visitor is treated to an expansive view down into the hall, where the modelling of the side walls is reflected in the rippled ceiling, the blank walling of the hall enlivened by the batik paintings by Thetis Blacker (**148**). The views beyond are superb, out to the lake, here very effectively brought right up to the building. With hindsight, the modesty of the entrance only serves to heighten the splendour of the interior, which is least expected.

Middleton uses the great change in levels here to create a lower vehicular service road, over which a pedestrian bridge leads to the new college. This is entered through a low entrance vestibule fronting a single-storey range with a copper mansard roof, a very unassuming entrance, because so much of the college is concealed on lower ground. But a surprise awaits, because the entrance level emerges onto a gallery at the upper level of the dining hall. At once

The lakeside path takes a more naturalistic line as it snakes away from the college, toward South Road, past the neat Principal's House. The path leads on through waist-high rushes and reeds, to a place where, looking back, the dining hall seems to sit floating magically on the water (**149**). In a design that is wholly contemporary, Phillip Middleton succeeded in bringing brick, leaf and water together to create a fine late twentieth-century landscape.

ELVET HILL AND THE ORIENTAL MUSEUM

Elvet Hill was the home of the architect Ignatius Bonomi. His stay was brief, and it remained a private house until the mid-twentieth century when it was bought by the university. The School of Oriental Studies moved in, its growing library and collection of Oriental objects blossoming into a museum of international importance, that now includes some of the finest examples of the arts of China and Ancient Egypt to be seen anywhere in Europe (**150**). To display these treasures, a major extension was completed in 1960.

Ignatius Bonomi (1787–1870) was the most celebrated architect of the early nineteenth century in County Durham. The son of an Italian architect, Ignatius arrived in Durham following his appointment as Durham County Bridge Surveyor in 1813. Over the following decades, as his architectural practice grew, he became one of that group of professional young men who

Oriental Museum – a view of the extension. (150)

espoused progressive causes in the city, such as the broadening of educational provision and prison reform. He joined the new Subscription Library on the corner of Owengate, and was a founder member of (and designed) the Mechanics' Institute in Claypath. When the university was founded in 1832, he was one of those privileged to use its new library. He mixed in the right circles, and counted amongst his friends the artist Joseph Bouet, the reformer Revd WS Gilly, the antiquarian, Revd

Oriental Museum – the original Elvet Hill house, designed and occupied by the architect Ignatius Bonomi. (151)

James Raine, and one of the founders of the university, Revd Temple Chevalier. He designed well over 100 buildings, including Lambton Castle, Eggleston Hall, Stanhope Rectory and Burn Hall.

By 1827 Bonomi was sufficiently established to build his own modest Durham country seat at Elvet Hill (**151**). The two-storey house combined his own domestic accommodation with his professional offices and is designed in a Tudor Gothic style – a solid and handsome house, well-proportioned, but nothing extravagant or ostentatious, very much a design that reflected the man.

But within ten years he had moved onto the peninsula. He sold Elvet Hill to the Fogg-Elliotts, who may have commissioned Bonomi to enlarge the house, with an extra floor and side extensions. In place of Bonomi's quiet villa, the house, with its steeply pitched roof and larger windows, took on a grander air.

The house remained in private hands until 1955 when the university acquired it for the School of Oriental Studies. The school had been set up in 1951 with Professor Thomas W Thacker as its first Director. Although its original purpose had been to teach the modern languages of the Near and Far East, Thacker was adamant that language teaching must be complemented by an understanding of material culture, stating that 'An Oriental School which aims to teach the cultural background of the oriental peoples must have a museum'.[32] By good chance at the same time, the then duke of Northumberland was wishing to sell his family's collection of Ancient Egyptian and Mesopotamian antiquities; the university moved fast and the collection came to Durham, where it grew.

The pressure to create a purpose-built museum received a huge boost in 1957 when the Gulbenkian Foundation donated £60,000 towards what became the Gulbenkian Museum of Oriental Art and Archaeology. The university appointed a local Middlesbrough practice, Philip R Middleton & Partners, as architects for the new building.

Middleton's building (actually the first phase of a larger museum[33]) was completed in 1960. Outwardly it is just a plain brick box with a narrow hipped roof, set into the sloping ground. As Elizabeth Williamson noted, it has none of the external display of a nineteenth-century museum. The two-storey interior is roofed with a space deck, with galleries around all sides looking over the main double-storey display area (**152**).

In 1983 a further extension was planned and an architectural competition held. The competition was won by Trevor Horne Associates, and matters progressed in 1995 when planning consent was obtained, but the extension was never built. In 2000 the Oriental Museum underwent a substantial reordering to provide a new mezzanine floor in the main exhibition hall, and in 2009 gallery displays were renewed.

Interior of the Oriental Museum. (152)

ST AIDAN'S COLLEGE

Ask anyone in Britain 50 years ago to name a famous architect, and you would hear just one name, time and again. Not Le Corbusier, Aalto or Wright ... but Spence. Sir Basil Spence was the architect of the new Coventry Cathedral, that icon of post-war architecture, a symbol of reconciliation and renewal. In Durham, he was the architect of the new St Aidan's College, and he gave the city a great building, albeit one that he would claim was never finished.

Female 'home students', were first admitted to Durham University in 1895. Their numbers were always small up to World War II, then grew rapidly.[34] In response, St Aidan's Society was created in 1947 to represent their interests and to provide communal facilities, the same year that Shincliffe Hall was acquired for some of their number.[35] By 1948 there were 94 students, now with a Common Room at 44 North Bailey.[36]

The principle of a new college for St Aidan's Society (it became a college in 1961), south of the city, was agreed in 1953, but nothing happened for five years.[37] By June 1959 the university had agreed that St Aidan's would be the next college to be built, providing accommodation for 200 women students. Three sites were shortlisted, the college preferring that between Elvet Hill and Observatory Hill, on a prominence known as Windmill Hill (153).[38] As the experience of St Mary's College had demonstrated, government funding would not include a new chapel, so St Aidan's established a chapel fund and sought contributions.[39]

In January 1960 the university approached four architects, each well established but, surprisingly, none was noted for university buildings.[40] After the

The dining hall and garden at St Aidan's College. (153)

baroque-style St Mary's and traditional Grey, they were advised that St Aidan's and the university were 'leaning towards a modernistic treatment rather than a severely traditional one to which we have adhered so far'. The architects' collective lack of university work did, in the end, count and all failed to impress, one rejected architect being told that the university had changed its mind and 'thought they should go for a man who had already done a college'.[41]

Fresh advice was sought from Cambridge, and three far more suitable architects were approached

– Philip Middleton, Peter Chamberlin and Basil Spence. Middleton was the local man, then working on Durham's new Gulbenkian Museum extension. Peter Chamberlin, of Chamberlin, Powell & Bon, designed the acclaimed Golden Lane Estate in London and New Hall, Cambridge, and Sir Basil Spence was the architect of the new Coventry Cathedral and Sussex University. Spence

Sir Basil Spence's plan for St Aidan's College, showing dining hall and chapel on the central axis. (154)

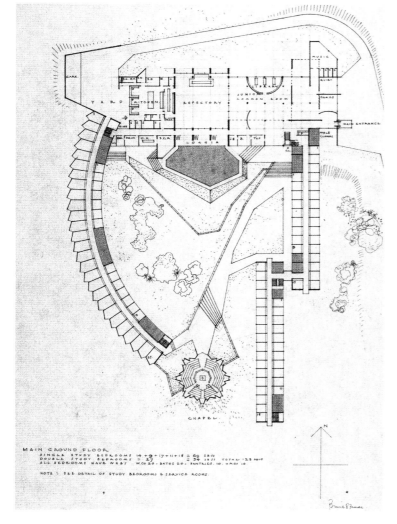

was already working for Durham University at Newcastle, designing the Physics Department's Herschel Building.

The college had wished that their new architect should be 'young and untraditional'.[42] At 53 Spence was scarcely young, but he was a modernist and a newly knighted one too. He was delighted to be appointed, telling the Warden, Sir James Duff, that 'nothing could be more interesting than to soak in the atmosphere of Durham and produce something of our own age exactly as the Chapel of Nine Altars was added to the nave [sic] of Durham Cathedral. At least one can aim at that sort of thing'.[43] It was an inspired appointment – the university and the college very much got the 'man of the moment'.

He began with the traditional concept of a college as buildings grouped around a central communal space, and went further in defining a north-south axis through his college to link the principal buildings – the dining hall (then called the refectory) and chapel, set at opposite ends of his courtyard – food for body and soul (**154**). (Spence could never have made the fine cathedral panorama central to his planning as it is angled to the site, but he did ensure that the view can be had from the library and the terrace.) As Spence's plans evolved, Sir James must have spoken with him about them, particularly concerning the unfunded chapel, as in August 1960 he cautioned him 'it would obviously be a mistake to plan a college around a building which can never be large and may be quite a long time before being built at all'.[44] Wise and prophetic words, albeit that Spence ignored them.

The dining hall is the central feature of the communal building, monumental in scale and

Far left: *The central community buildings and garden at St Aidan's College.* (155)

Left: *The dining hall, St Aidan's College.* (156)

built with a reinforced concrete frame, clad in buff bricks, with three-bay fully glazed walls, north and south, set back behind brick piers (155). These piers support projecting concrete beams, arched below with a gentle segmental curve, a theme which is carried inside the hall with shallow timber-clad 'vaults', a form inspired perhaps by the great Roman ruins Spence saw around him while designing the British Embassy in Rome in the early 1960s. Elain Harwood has concluded, 'Only [at St Aidan's] does [Spence] repeat the strength and rigorous geometry found in his contemporary Sussex University … inspired by the idiom of Le Corbusier's Maisons Jaoul and the antique'.[45] The formal grandeur of the hall's interior is beautifully reinforced with paintings by Kirill Sokolov. The dining hall is the best of St Aidan's and the best of the South Road colleges' dining halls (156).

From the main communal buildings, two wings of student accommodation run south, the western curving, its wall saw-toothed to bring sunlight to each room. The eastern wing is straight but doglegs, and includes the library. Both residential wings have traditional long corridors, a plan form

retained despite some criticism at the time from the University Grants Committee (157).[46]

The central courtyard garden introduces new geometry, neither orthogonal or curved, but asymmetrical and sharp, its hard angles softened by Brian Hackett's landscaping (158).

The southern focal point in Spence's design was the chapel, intended to be a centrally planned, star-shaped building, its walls powerfully modelled with slit windows concealed in the folds. He had

Western residential wing, St Aidan's College. (157)

Above: *The central garden, St Aidan's College.* (158)

Below: *Sir Basil Spence's sketch for the proposed chapel, St Aidan's College.* (159)

a meeting-house or concert hall, if only he can have it as an architectural feature) and invited the audience to give him £25,000 for it'.[48] Sadly the money never came, the chapel was never built and St Aidan's is the poorer without it.

St Aidan's was begun on site in 1962 and completed in 1964, designed through Spence's Edinburgh office, Spence, Glover & Ferguson. His original plan did not provide detached staff accommodation and subsequently these were added (post 1966) on the eastern side of the entrance drive, set against the trees. A little later in 1973, came the Principal's House, a very neat L-shaped design in buff brick, by Robin Dower of architects Spence & Price.

In 1981 the college became mixed, and was also extended a year later.[49] Faulkner-Brown, Hendy, Watkinson & Stonor's 42–bedroom extension is now D, E, F and G Houses.[50] The new building left Spence's plan untouched, running

produced similar designs for the side chapels at Coventry Cathedral (**159**).[47] With no government funding and little in the college's chapel fund, it was never built. It was left to Sir Basil at the opening ceremony to plead for funding, as one witness recalled: 'the architect spoke, about his chapel (which he is now quite ready to turn into

PERSPECTIVE LOOKING FROM LOGGIA

south from its east wing. The design has a clever duality about, reflecting each elevation's principal purpose. To the east, beside the public entrance drive, the elevation impresses with rippled waves of metal sheet and continuous windows. To the west, more privately, all is domestic brick with individual entrances, overhanging eaves, and more than a nod at Erskine's Byker housing in East Newcastle upon Tyne (**160**).

The same duality is evident in the further additions of 1992, designed by Howarth Litchfield Partnership, essentially following where Faulkner-Brown had led, but with a more menacing external face, each floor coming forward rather than receding. The same architects added the curving Lindisfarne Centre (1993) around the unbuilt chapel site. The latest additions to the college have been the entrance and social space (2008–9) in the east wing, by PH Partnership.

INSTITUTE FOR MIDDLE EAST AND ISLAMIC STUDIES AND DURHAM BUSINESS SCHOOL

To the east, at the foot of St Aidan's College, on Elvet Hill Road is the Institute for Middle East and Islamic Studies, (2002–3, Howarth Litchfield Partnership) (**161**). To the west of the college lies the Durham Business School, once cruciform, now quadrangular due to later additions. The original building of 1977–8 is by William Whitfield with a long range of three linked pavilions, each with a buttressed basement, supporting an upper storey of tall glazing lights between thick mullions of dark brown aggregate. The themes of some of his earlier university buildings are all there – a strong articulation of each element, military references and powerful, if sombre, character (**162**). Major additions are underway at the time of writing (GSS Architecture).

Left: *Durham University Business School.* (162)

Below: *The Observatory.* (163)

Opposite (left): *The later Faulkner-Brown-designed residential wing, St Aidan's College.* (160)

Opposite (right): *Institute for Middle East and Islamic Studies.* (161)

OBSERVATORY AND OBELISK

Theoretical astronomy was taught in the university from 1835, supervised by the Professor of Mathematics, the Revd Temple Chevalier.[51] In 1838 the university acquired astronomical instruments from the noted amateur astronomer, the Revd T J Hussey.[52] The decision to build the Observatory followed, Chevalier raising the funding from private subscription with university and diocesan support.[53]

The new building was designed by Anthony Salvin and completed by June 1840, when the instruments were ready to be installed.[54] Principal amongst them was a Fraunhofer Refractor equatorial telescope, one of the best in Europe at the time.[55] Observations began by the end of 1840, ending only in 1937.[56]

Salvin, freed perhaps from the Gothic constraints of the peninsula, designed a neat, well-proportioned classical building, with a square plan ground floor, where the observer lived, above which rises a Greek cross first floor with extended arms.[57] The observational equipment was here, with a copper dome rising above (**163**).

In 1850, W L Wharton of Dryburn, at his own expense, erected an obelisk in the grounds of his house to serve as a North Meridian Mark for the Observatory. This still stands in the grounds of St Leonard's RC comprehensive school, off North Road.[58] No architect is known, though Salvin must be a possible candidate.

SOUTH ROAD: EAST

GREY COLLEGE

Durham University was discussing plans for a new college for 200 men as far back as the early 1940s[1], and by 1949 a site was identified above Little High Wood.[2] By the end of that year, Prof. J S Allen had prepared the plans, though his assistant, the young William Whitfield, was probably the architect, as he was designing the West Building (Lower Mountjoy) at the same time (**164**). The scheme was reaffirmed in a 1952 report, as the new college was intended to accommodate young scientists studying at the enlarged applied science courses the university planned.[3] Despite this aspiration, funding limitations prevented the scheme progressing for a further four years.

In 1956 the scheme was revived, but by then both site and architect had changed. The site had moved down to Fountains Field, a steeply sloping field south of Hollingside Lane with magnificent views of the cathedral. The new architects were Thomas Worthington & Sons, already tackling the university's redevelopments in Owengate and North Bailey.[4] Worthingtons, a traditionalist practice, had also designed student accommodation at Leicester University.[5]

Building in Durham in the 1950s was a complex process of consultation, not just with two local authorities, but with City Council consultant

The central green, Grey College. (165)

Thomas Sharp and, via the County Council, the Royal Fine Arts Commission. The initial Worthington plan was considered unacceptable because it brought the buildings too close together, cutting out cathedral views (**165**). A revised plan kept the buildings apart and, at Sharp's particular insistence, the open view from Hollingside Lane was preserved.[6] Cost constraints also meant the college had to be built in brick, not stone.[7]

Work finally began on site on the west range (Elvet) in 1957 and a year later the new college was named after Charles, 2nd Earl Grey, Prime Minister of the Reform Act in 1832, the year

Above: *J S Allen (William Whitfield) design for the first 'Grey' college at Upper Mountjoy, 1949.* (164)

Right: *The dining hall, Hollingside, Grey College.* (166)

of the university's foundation.[8] (His statue by Thomas Campbell, 1838, stands in Hollingside.)

In March 1959, as work approached completion on Elvet, a disastrous fire swept through the building, destroying much of the interior. Amazingly, the building was reroofed, repaired and opened on time in September. Little wonder the phoenix was adopted as the college symbol thereafter.

Work on the main building (Hollingside) began in November 1959 and was completed in October 1961 (**166**).[9] Grey's third accommodation block, Oswald, south of Hollingside Lane, was opened in late 1963.

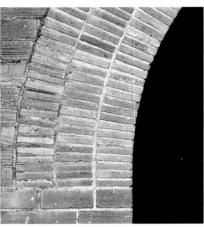

Far left: *The view to the cathedral, Grey College.* (167)

Left: *The superb brick detailing at Grey College.* (168)

Below: *The chapel in Fountains Hall, Grey College.* (169)

The completed college garnered the kind of polite architectural criticism that, if it fell short of outright praise, neither did it condemn. The *Architectural Review* in 1960 said it had a 'washed-out contemporary style'. Elizabeth Williamson remarked that it looked like 'a mature suburban housing estate'.[10] Even the first Master could only manage 'reasonably satisfactory'.[11]

Worthington's Grey College is not great architecture, but neither is it a poor building. As improved by Sharp's intervention, its layout – of buildings set out around a wide grass slope, closed at one end by a great stand of trees and at the other by the cathedral – works brilliantly (**167**). It creates that particular enclosure, by buildings, nature and panorama, that is the signature of so many Durham colleges.

Look more closely at the buildings themselves and you will see restful elevations and tidy courts. Take time to look at the fine brick-tiled lintels and arches and marvel at how they were crafted (**168**). Here in the details lie much of the building's worth, and future care must protect, and restore that fine-grained quality.

Inside there are good spaces, many of them plainly walled – ideal for displaying Grey's substantial art collection, impressive even by the standards seen throughout the university.

The need for a multi-purpose building, for a chapel and meeting hall, was first mooted in 1965, intended for the site of an old cottage in Hollingside Lane. Architect Harold Wharfe's first scheme was twice the estimated cost, so, when finished in 1971, Fountains Hall was much cheaper and on a new site, south of High Close (now the Master's House). Economy was not achieved at the cost of quality; this is a clever building, tidying disparate functions under the unity of a great asymmetrical pyramid roof. The chapel is a little gem, with its freely curving walls and slit windows; its bare surfaces, like so much at Grey's, adorned with art (**169**).

Later architects at Grey's followed Wharfe's example in giving the college's quiet courts additions with a stronger voice. The SCR dining room (Pennington Room) of 1978–9, designed by Dennis Jones, raised a wing of Hollingside an extra storey to provide a dramatic fully glazed gable. Howarth Litchfield Partnership's Holgate

House (1993–5) shouts even louder, a tall accommodation range, high on the hillside, with strongly coloured brickwork and replete with post-modernist references. The same practice's JCR extension, completed in 2012, is a much more contextual affair, nicely buttressing the dining hall and very successfully picking up on Worthington's materials and details.

COLLINGWOOD COLLEGE

Collingwood College has no visual link to the Durham peninsula. Unlike St Mary's or Grey's colleges, massing buildings to frame views towards the eyecatcher of the cathedral was not an option for its designers. But its site was once the gardens and parkland of a large country seat, Oswald House, and around it there remained a mature landscape of large trees. How the college architect succeeded in responding to those trees with a powerful building that brings the built and natural landscapes harmoniously together, is very much Collingwood's story.[12]

The original Oswald House, later the site of Collingwood College. (170)

In 1960, the University Grants Committee (UGC) asked all universities to prepare development plans for the period after 1963. Durham's response was to propose three new colleges (X, Y and Z), two men's and one women's, and a new building for St Aidan's College *(see 'Trevelyan College' for full details)*. College 'Y' was to become Collingwood College. Planned for 350 men, it was initially deferred until after 1961 due to public expenditure cuts.[13]

The university's plan for the South Road colleges, as revised in 1962, showed college 'Y' on the Oswald House estate, but retaining the house itself for university use. Oswald House had been built about 1830 by the Wilkinson family and later acquired by the Sadler family. In May 1950 Mrs Amy Sadler sold the estate to the university retaining a life tenancy, relinquished when she left in 1963.

The house was approached from South Road, past a small lodge, up a winding tree-lined carriage drive to the top of the hill, to the NW front of the long stone villa (**170**). The main garden front looked out over grounds sloping to the SW, down to a large open meadow in which was an irregular pond and two distant tree clumps.

The university's wish to hold an architectural competition was declined by the UGC, who recommended a direct appointment. In July 1963 Richard Sheppard of Richard Sheppard Robson Partnership was appointed, no doubt very much on his reputation for the much-lauded Churchill College, Cambridge, completed three years earlier.

Sheppard produced his first scheme in December 1963. It was illustrated in the *Architectural Review* in 1965, and showed the old house demolished and on its site a new communal building from which four residential clusters sprang, two down the southern slopes and two to the north. The floor plan of each cluster had a central stair, with four wings, each of six bedrooms. The southern clusters, being on sloping land, could be accessed on an upper floor, with floors above and below, making them appear less tall. The use of a cluster plan with short corridors was considered an improvement over the traditionally long corridor plans, not favoured by the UGC, but used at Van Mildert and St Aidan's, although the architects at Trevelyan were developing similar short-cluster blocks at the same time. There was some university debate over the loss of the house, but all parties finally accepted it, and in 1965 it was demolished.

In 1966, the UGC changed tack suggesting Durham expand existing colleges rather than build new ones. The university's response, faced with financial constraints, planners' concerns over building heights (Sheppard's first proposal had seven-storey clusters) and thoughts about phasing the scheme, all prompted a redesign in February 1968. The new scheme was lower, simpler and cheaper. From the communal block, with dining hall, public rooms, JCR etc, still sited where the house had stood, two residential wings ran south down the slope, each with groups of linked staircases. The eastern wing was four storeys high with six staircases, the western wing five storeys with three staircases. There were ten study bedrooms off each landing. As in the earlier scheme the retention of trees from the former estate was critical in separating the residential blocks from each other, and ensuring privacy between rooms. The design was also adjusted for mixed student use (**171**).

The college in the trees, Collingwood College. (171)

Planning permission was sought late in 1968, the only snag from the County Planning Office being the architect's choice of cherry-red bricks, which were conditioned on the planning approval. During the preparation of detailed constructional drawings and tendering, a prolonged debate followed. Two and a half years later, the brick was finally agreed – a Crossley's 'Dark Heather' – a

The Principal's house, Collingwood College. (172)

choice, it should be noted, not unlike Trevelyan's brick and a colour much admired and used by the university's consultant architect William Whitfield on his own buildings. Loyalties were evidently strained: as an Estates and Buildings Officer remarked at the time, 'the [university's] Buildings Committee were somewhat innocent bystanders in the controversy, backing their architect to the hilt but hoping the County Planning Officer would win'. Work began in August 1971, the college was part occupied in 1973, and completed the following year (**172**).

College Y was subsequently named after Sir Edward Collingwood (1900–70), an eminent mathematician and Chairman of the Council of Durham University at the time. The stag from the Collingwood coat of arms became the college symbol.

Brian Hackett, the university's consultant landscape architect, was appointed to work with Sheppard on the design of the grounds, endorsing the view that as many trees as possible should be kept. They also carefully landscaped the old pond and the surrounding meadowland. The college won a Northern RIBA award in 1974, praised for its skilful use of sloping site, preservation of trees, and effective use of brick and timber (**173**).

Sheppard and Hackett deserve special praise for their work at Collingwood. In summer the college is hidden from view, barely rising above the wooded edge, south of the city. Trees embrace it, frame it, mark its entrances and exits, both in the grand approach from South Road, and in the narrow accidental path that leads down to the near-perfect, touch-it-at-your peril, paddock (**174**). These are not the young trees of Trevelyan, but

Below: *The trees ensure privacy, Collingwood College.* (173)

Below right: *The beckoning light of the paddock, Collingwood College.*(174)

big trees that signal an older landscape. Against such giants, Richard Sheppard was able to make a correspondingly strong architectural response. His residential blocks are the most powerful elements in the design, and share with Trevelyan College a love of simple well-detailed brickwork perforated with deeply recessed dark windows, notably on the corners – another trait it shares with Trevelyan.

In the 1990s the government again encouraged universities to expand, and at Durham each college was to draw up a strategic plan for 1992–7. Collingwoods's preferred option of accommodating 200 students in new buildings in the paddock was opposed by the City Planning Office. Subsequently, architect Sheila Hyland of RPS Clouston was approached. The new buildings were required to look similar to the original college, with new residential and conference facilities to be provided. Work started in June 1993 and was completed October 1994, adding 230 students to the college.

BOTANIC GARDEN

The university's Botanic Garden was first established in 1925 after the completion of the Science Laboratories (Dawson Building) at what is now Lower Mountjoy. As the Science site gradually developed over succeeding decades, the garden was always under threat, so that in 1969 the university transferred it to its present site. This was formerly the outer gardens and farmland of Hollingside House and here, in expansive grounds, the garden could be re-established and grow, free from development pressure. In 1971 planting the new garden began in earnest.

Following development on the Howlands Farm site (now Ustinov and Josephine Butler colleges) in the 1990s, the boundaries of the

The Visitor Centre, Botanic Garden. (175)

garden were enlarged and now cover 10 hectares (25 acres). The visitor centre was built in 1988 (RPS Clouston) (**175**). With the establishment of the Durham Park and Ride Interchange, SW of the Garden, a new entrance, direct from the car park, was created in 2005 (PH Partnership).

Much of the garden around the northern part of the site, around the visitor centre, has an exposed slope to the SW which receives the full force of the prevailing winds. Here have been planted British and European species.

South of the visitor centre are the two glasshouses containing cacti and tropical plants. Close by are smaller beds devoted to Ethnobotany, Fossil Fern and South African Collections, a Plant History Bed and an Alpine Garden.

Further south stands a mature monkey puzzle tree (*Araucaria araucana)* a reminder of the period when this area of the garden was part of the wider landscaped grounds of Hollingside House (**176**). Near this tree is a commemorative stone, erected by the Roberts family who lived there, to Major Frederick John Roberts, who died in World War I and is buried in France.

East of Hollingside House itself is the Oriental Collection, within which stands the Vessels of Life Sculpture and the Sakura Friendship Garden of flowering cherries.

Running west, towards South Road is an extensive North American arboretum. Nine different woodlands have been planted to represent the major forest types of North America.

Below the North American arboretum, on steeper slopes leading into a valley is the Himalayan Collection, where the planting here reflects the plant associations found in Nepal at 3,000–4,000m altitude (**177**).

Beyond the woodland cover, on the open ground adjoining Ustinov and Josephine Butler colleges, a pinetum was planted out in 2010. In the adjacent field, a wildflower meadow was established, grazed in the traditional way by the university's own herd of rare Manx Loaghtan sheep.

Left: *Hollingside House and ha-ha.* (178)

Below: *Hollingside House in its garden setting.* (179)

HOLLINGSIDE HOUSE

Hollingside House, now the home of the Vice-Chancellor of the university, was once a small country house with extensive gardens, part of which now lies within the Botanic Garden. The house developed from modest late eighteenth-century origins, first in stone, then brick. It has a fine walled garden, separated from its outer gardens by a ha-ha (**178**).[14] Variations in the brickwork suggest that part of the first house was single storey, later raised a storey (**179**). From 1850 to 1852 this was the home of Revd John Bacchus Dykes, the prolific hymn writer. He was Precentor of Durham Cathedral (1849–62), then vicar of St Oswald's church, Durham, until his death in 1876.[15] One of his best-known tunes is named after the house.

Community buildings, Josephine Butler College. (180)

JOSEPHINE BUTLER AND USTINOV COLLEGES

The Howlands Farm College, as it was first known, took the university campus far south, out of Durham and beyond the trees, into open countryside. The winner of the architectural competition for the new college aspired to establish something of a Tuscan hill town on the gentle southern slopes off South Road. At such a distance from the heart of the university on the peninsula, the new college might have seemed remote, but its architects radically reformed the landscape to give its students a view back to where the university began, at the foot of the cathedral (180).

The expansion of the university in the early 1990s led to a capacity study of the existing colleges. Primarily this meant looking at the South Road colleges in their generous parkland, rather than hoping to find more space for students on the tightly packed peninsula. The aesthetic problem was that those colleges enjoyed a balanced harmony between their buildings and landscape. Add too many buildings into green spaces and that special quality would be destroyed. There were also concerns that the social fabric of college life might suffer if they became too big; colleges of more than 1000 students were not thought right for Durham.

In the end, some limited expansion was possible in existing colleges, but they could not totally absorb the planned increase without risking both environmental and social damage. It was apparent that the university needed a new college if they were to reach their planned expansion target.

The university owned land south of the Botanic Garden, a beautiful site that rose to a gentle hill, then fell to the south and east, down to a valley set against the deep woodland behind Hollingside. The area was an Area of Great Landscape Value, so the university needed a very high-quality scheme. To achieve this they launched an architectural competition in 1994, determined 'to create something special in this special place'.[16]

The competition brief suggested a vision of a 'scholastic village', a community of people of different ages and backgrounds. It also required the buildings to have minimal visual impact on the landscape, anticipating a position on the lower slopes of the hill. It also asked for a green solution that would avoid major movement of spoil from the site and would also achieve low-energy consumption targets.

The competition was won by Arup Associates (James Burland, partner in charge).[17] Their scheme laid out a string of 21 housing clusters like a loose necklace around the upper slopes of the hill, with communal buildings on flatter ground towards South Road (**181**). Each cluster had two housing blocks, cranked at varying angles around a central hinge of the glazed staircase and a high timber-clad wind tower that would naturally ventilate the student rooms. It was these wind towers, and the irregular, organic feel to the housing clusters that evoked parallels with Tuscan hill towns.

Surplus spoil could have been used to infill the valley of the lower meadow slopes, but, in an inspired design decision, Burland chose instead to pile it up in the centre, on top of the shallow hill, to raise its summit. What was created was an artificial 'mount', very much the successor of Renaissance models, from which the necklace of college housing could be viewed below, while above, the cathedral rose on the skyline, thus linking this distant college along its entrance axis, back to the peninsula.

The scheme was a deserving winner, the architectural and landscape concept was both sympathetic and innovative. The first phase of post-graduate housing was eventually completed in 1999, with eight clusters built and a small amenity building fashioned out of an old brick barn (**182**). The ensemble established a sense of a hamlet, if not yet a full hill village, with simple landscaping flowing into the enclosed spaces, as natural extensions of the wildflower meadows beyond. Sadly one of the scheme's most distinctive features, its wind towers, proved (in a post-occupancy evaluation) to be unsustainable in its energy savings, and were not to appear again on the site (**183**).

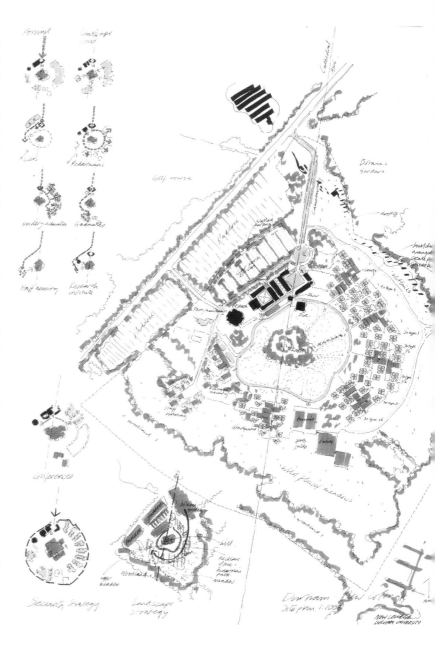

Arup Associates original 'Howlands Farm' college concept, with its strong landscape axis, linking the cathedral to the view from the central mount. Josephine Butler and Ustinov Colleges. (181)

Above: *The Phase One Arup housing, Josephine Butler and Ustinov colleges.* (182)

Right: *Detail of the Phase One Arup housing, Josephine Butler and Ustinov colleges.* (183)

After a short delay, the scheme progressed in 2003, with new architects, GSS Architecture, re-interpreting Arup's village clusters in larger and denser configurations of traditional housing blocks, still threaded with strong landscaping. The central college buildings were also redesigned on a radial layout, out from the central hill. The £35 million project, completed in 2006, provided accommodation for 1000 students in the postgraduate Ustinov College – named after Sir Peter Ustinov, the renowned actor and University Chancellor (1992–2004) – and Josephine Butler College (named after the nineteenth-century social reformer).

Once Josephine Butler College was occupied, its students warmed to their new home, loved its 'mount', and duly adopted the mole as the college mascot. James Burland would be well pleased.

MOVING THROUGH THE LANDSCAPE

The university is good walking territory. There is plenty to enjoy; an historic building, a sculpture, a cathedral panorama, an ancient tree. These features demand that you stand and stop and enjoy them, taking in their detail, their composition, fixed to the spot. But there are also those walking pleasures that invite you to continue your journey, to pass through a space, to move under an arch, kinetic delights that lead you on. This is Gordon Cullen's 'serial vision' in action. It is the beckoning vision of Claude's landscapes, through darkness to light, and in Durham it happens in the most unsuspecting places. You just find yourself drawn onwards … wanting to explore.

Above left: *College gate to the Bailey.* (184)

Left: *The chapel arches, Hatfield College.* (185)

Above: *Steps are invariably inviting. The riverbank terrace and castle wall at Hatfield College.* (186)

Right: *The sequence of gardens behind St Chad's College.* (187)

Overleaf: *Onwards into the light, Kingsgate Bridge and Bow Lane.* (188)

STOCKTON AND USHAW

QUEEN'S CAMPUS, STOCKTON-ON-TEES

Origins

It was the Vice-Chancellor of Durham University, Professor Fred Holliday who, in the mid-1980s, first conceived of the idea of a university campus on Teesside.[1] The concept, of what was to become Queen's Campus, was more formally set down in 1987, the same year as Prime Minister Margaret Thatcher took her famous 'walk in the wilderness' at Stockton. Later, in Durham, she gave the Vice-Chancellor confidential support for his Teesside base.[2]

When the Teesside Development Corporation (TDC) was established soon after, the university found a ready ear. There were obvious advantages for both parties. For the university it represented the opportunity for expansion, which was increasingly physically constrained in Durham itself, and it also offered new sources of external funding. For the TDC it offered a prestigious university investing in an area badly needing additional higher educational provision.

The academic direction of the new campus was set towards offering degrees on Environmental Sciences, Human Sciences and European Studies, with plans to encourage the development of a research centre in those disciplines. This was to be accommodated in the Phase 1 teaching building, with students accommodated nearby. Similar buildings were to be provided in Phase 2, along with a research centre.

The Holliday Building, Queen's Campus, Stockton. (189)

Queen's Campus buildings

The focus for Queen's Campus is the teaching buildings on the south side of a broad stretch of the River Tees, close to the centre of Stockton, strictly speaking in Thornaby-on-Tees. The first was the Holliday Building, opened in 1992, designed by Halliday Meecham Architects (**189**). This is a strongly articulated building with a handsome central rotunda, from which three hammer-headed arms stretch out, that runs to the riverside curving into a great arc as it hugs the river's edge. As with all the teaching buildings on the campus, the walls are clad in fair-faced concrete blockwork, with shallow metal flat roofs. The building is generously glazed and quite reminiscent of early modernism in style. The colour of it all is warm buff-grey, a mood-changing colour that can really lift the spirits in bright sunshine, but can chill on a dull day.

To complement this first-phase teaching building, student housing of 234 ensuite bedrooms was opened in 1994 (Fletcher Joseph, architects). In 2001 these buildings became the core of John Snow College, a cluster of brick blocks, set back away from the river.

The second phase of Queen's Campus was marked by the opening in 1998 of the Ebsworth Building, a teaching building, designed by Dennis Lister & Associates (**190**). The main L-plan block is neatly articulated at its ends with shallow pitched roofs and full-height canted glazed bays. It has the same palette of materials as the Holliday Building, relieved here by a little banded brickwork. It is impressive despite its inland setting. The same year, 203 new student rooms were completed nearby, also designed by Dennis Lister & Associates, with a further 80 finished the following year. This later

became Stephenson College. A new JCR opened in 2010 (GSS architects). Nearby, the Team Durham Sports Centre opened in the same year.

If the Ebsworth Building failed to make the water's edge, the preferred site was perhaps already allocated to the new research centre – the Wolfson Research Building – which provided laboratories, offices and a seminar room. It opened in 2001 and was designed by The Austin Company, with a fourth wing added in 2012 (GSS Architects)

There is a sense in which this represents the most powerful of the Queen's Campus buildings and the

Wolfson Research Building, Queen's Campus, Stockton. (191)

one that best reflects its site's character and history (**191**). To the river side, three tall concrete fins are set between a low, quadrant-curved, metal-roofed building. It is a surprisingly simple but bold design, something absolutely right for the scale of industrial Teesside, making a great silhouette in this big-skied landscape. Here, perhaps, the *genius loci* of the Teesside site has been best understood, a taste of what in Middlesbrough they call the 'land of giants'.

Such fine riverside elevations were given greater prominence by the construction in 2007–8 of another giant, the Infinity Bridge (Expedition Engineering, lead designers), a spectacular dual bowstring bridge comprising a pair of continuous, differently sized structural steel arches with a suspended pedestrian deck (**192**). Though not

university-funded, it brings great practical benefit to Queen's Campus, linking it to the North Shore Redevelopment Project. It also brings real glamour.

The Infinity Bridge, Queen's Campus, Stockton. (192)

USHAW COLLEGE

Durham University has long enjoyed a close association with the Roman Catholic Seminary at Ushaw College, just three miles (5km) west of Durham. One of its residential blocks officially became a Hall of the university in 1968. With the closure of the college in June 2011, the Trustees (the bishops of the Northern Province and Shrewsbury Diocese) established a project group to oversee a development strategy for the whole college site, and invited the university to commission a joint feasibility study to consider future options.

In the short term, Durham Business School will relocate to Ushaw for two years while major extension and refurbishment works are carried out to the school's premises in Durham. The university is also undertaking the substantial task of updating, to modern standards, the cataloguing of the books and archives in Ushaw Library, one of the largest and most important Catholic libraries in the country. It has also been agreed that the Trustees and Durham University will work together to establish an Ushaw Centre for Catholic Scholarship and Heritage.

As the relationship between the university and Ushaw develops more closely, it is fitting to give an outline, albeit briefly, of the great cultural wealth of the college.

An aerial view of the main buildings at Ushaw College. (193)

Ushaw College has its roots in the foundation of the English College at Douai in 1568, for the training of English Catholic priests. Forced to leave in 1795 after the French Revolution, the college came to County Durham and finally settled at Ushaw in 1799. The first Seminary buildings (1804–8), laid out in three ranges around a central court, were designed by James Taylor, a prominent Catholic architect (**193**). A fourth range was added by 1819 and the south range was raised in 1907 (**194**). This was the one and only classical building at Ushaw, all that followed was Gothic.

At first there was little growth in college numbers, the great expansion began in 1847, and by the end of the century the college was three times its original size, with new buildings arranged around a series of courts. The eminent Victorian architect, Augustus Welby Northmore Pugin, designed a new chapel (1844–7) to the east of the college, but this quickly became inadequate for the growing seminary and it was replaced in 1884 by one designed by Dunn & Hansom, 'in most respects a reproduction of the old', but twice the size (**195**). The new chapel is on a magnificent scale, richly decorated and furnished and incorporating a number of features and furnishings from its 1847 predecessor. In the main college, the old chapel was remodelled and Gothicised as an Exhibition Hall in 1848 by Joseph Hansom. AWN Pugin also remodelled the old refectory there.

To the west of the old college, a large library was built in 1849–51 (Charles & Joseph Hansom), planned to complement the original Pugin Chapel to the east. To the north, A W N Pugin designed the Stations Cloister and associated chapels in 1852–3. Only St Charles' Chapel (1857–9) is by his son, Edward Welby Pugin, who was also the architect of the small mortuary chapel (1858–9) with its exceptionally fine altar and reredos carving.

E W Pugin designed many more of Ushaw's buildings, including the Chemical Laboratory (1854–6) and the large, and sadly derelict, Junior Seminary and St Aloysius Chapel (1857–9) west of the main group. To the east of the college lies the extraordinary Bounds Wall with three large ball courts and six racket houses laid out in a great oval, the setting for Ushaw's unique games (Joseph Hansom, *c*.1860).

This short summary of Ushaw's wonderful assembly of buildings, all set in generous gardens and parkland, serves only to highlight the unique heritage that must find a new future. It is a story, as they say, 'to be continued … '.

Opposite: *The main chapel at Ushaw College.* (195)

Below: *The original college buildings, Ushaw College.* (194)

APPENDIX: ENDNOTES | A

CHAPTER 2

1. JT Fowler, *Durham University: Earlier Foundations and Present Colleges,* 1904, 23.

2. Durham University Library, Special Collections; Durham University Collections; Introductory notes.

3. CE Whiting, *The University of Durham, 1832-1932,* Sheldon Press, 1932.

4. *Ibid,* Whiting.

5. *Op cit,* Fowler.

6. H Tudor, *St Cuthbert's Society*, 2.

7. *Op cit,* Fowler, 34.

8. *Op cit,* Tudor, 4.

9. DULSC UND/F8/C1/E6 University Building Committee Minutes, 11 Jan 1949.

10. *Op cit,* Tudor, 166.

11. *Northern Architect,* 12, Sept/Oct 1963, 5.

12. S Martin, *Trevs: A Celebration of 40 Years of Trevelyan College, Durham,* 2006, 88.

CHAPTER 3

1. CE Whiting, *Nathaniel, Lord Crewe, Bishop of Durham (1674-1721) and his Diocese,* 1940.

2. Bishop's coach house by Salvin, presumably also 1841. See E Cambridge, 'Book Review of J Allibone's Anthony Salvin: Pioneer of Gothic Revival Architecture', *Durham Archaeological Journal,* 4, 1988, 69–73. Also Durham Cathedral Chapter Library DCD/N/CA/AD14/1-8, Salvin Drawings.

3. N Pevsner, *Buildings of England: County Durham,* 2nd edition, 1983, 243.

4. *Ibid,* Pevsner.

5. Durham University Library, Special Collections; Durham University Collections; Introductory notes.

6. BISHOP COSIN'S LIBRARY BIBLIOGRAPHY:

    CE Whiting, 'Cosin's Library', *Transactions of the Architectural and Archaeological Society of Durham and Northumberland,* 9, 1939–43, 18–32.

    JDT Hall, 'Cosin's Library' in M Johnson (ed), *John Cosin: From Priest to Prince Bishop,* 91–8.

    G Ornsby (ed), *The Correspondence of John Cosin, D.D., Lord Bishop of Durham,* Surtees Society, 52, 55, 1869 and 1872.

    AI Doyle, 'John Cosin (1595-1672) as a Library Maker', *The Book Collector,* 40, 3, 1991.

    D Ramage, 'The Library Buildings on Palace Green', *Durham University Journal,* June 1946. 94–100.

    Peter Pace, *The Architecture of George Pace, 1915-75,* 1990.

    D Ramage, 'Bishop Cosin's Library: Restoration 1958', *Transactions of the Architectural and Archaeological Society of Durham and Northumberland,* 11, 1962, 292–4.

    D Ramage, 'Portrait Heads for Cosin's Library', *Transactions of the Architectural and Archaeological Society of Durham and Northumberland,* 1965, 461–4.

7. *GSS Architecture, Heritage Statement,* to accompany Alteration and Refurbishment Proposals for Palace Green Library, n.d, c.2011.

8. Hut clearance note by Dr Ian Doyle, pers comm.

9. David Watkinson notes, via Dr Sheila Hingley, pers comm.

10. D Ramage, 'The Library Buildings on Palace Green', *Durham University Journal,* June 1946. 94–100.

11. *Ibid,* 97.

12. AI Doyle, 'John Cosin (1595-1672) as a Library Maker', *The Book Collector,* 40, 3, 1991.

13. CE Whiting, 'Cosin's Library', *Transactions of the Architectural and Archaeological Society of Durham and Northumberland,* 9, 1939–43, 19.

14. 1880s according to Dr Ian Doyle, pers comm.

15. *Op cit,* Doyle.

16. Dr Ian Doyle suggests he hung full-length portraits of English bishops.

17. *Ibid,* Doyle.

18. DULSC UND/EA1/B3/1-2.

19. Peter Pace, *The Architecture of George Pace, 1915-75,* 1990, 229–30 (Full list of architectural works).

20. Elain Harwood, English Heritage Building Report: Palace Green Library (Pace Building), unpublished.

CHAPTER 4

1. A painted ceiling was discovered here during renovation work, offered to, but not taken by, The Bowes Museum.

2. P Ryder, *Durham Buildings Survey,* 101.

3. N Pevsner, *Buildings of England: County Durham,* 2nd edition, 1983, 242.

4. Dr Ian Doyle, pers comm.

5. George Pickering's drawings of 1847: DCD/N/CA /AD/49/1-22 and 50/1-19. Pevsner gives building completion date of 1851.

6. Jo Jones, *Durham Theatre* leaflets for Durham Heritage Centre, *c.*1990.

7. Remodelled 1949-50, 'both inside and outside to form a charming little theatre' – *St Mary's College Newsletter,* 1949–50, 4.

8. W A Moyes, *Hatfield 1846-1996: A History of Hatfield College in the University of Durham,* 1996, 6.

9. *Ibid,* Moyes.

10. H Tudor, *St Cuthbert's Society,* 2.

11. T A Whitworth, *Yellow Sandstone and Mellow Brick: An account of Hatfield College, Durham, 1846-1971,* 17. Also the venue for music concerts by John Garth, the Durham Composer, Prof. Tim Burt, pers comm.

12. *Ibid,* Whitworth.

13. Whitworth gives a detailed account of ownerships, from 1660 to 1845.

14. Heath was living at North Bailey in 1642, but had moved to Old Durham by 1648.

15. 1st Edition Ordnance Survey Map, 1857.

16. *Op cit,* Moyes, 27.

17. *Ibid,* 27. Also Prof Tim Burt, Master pers comm., who suggests Thorpe more likely than Bishop Maltby, despite disagreement between Melville and Thorp, as Melville was ousted by the time the chapel was built.

18. *Ibid,* 45.

19. *Ibid,* 73.

20. *Op cit,* Whitworth, 26.

21. Gazetteer site No 33. 'City of Durham Archaeological Survey', *Durham Archaeological Journal,* 9, 1993, 38.

22. *Op cit,* Moyes, 247.

23. For a summary of the college's property acquisitions and swaps, see the DULSC introduction to its St Chad's College archive in Special Collections; Durham University Records: Colleges; St Chad's College. The history is fully documented in the annual St Chad's College Magazine.

24. *St Chad's College Magazine,* 1, 1938, 41. 'For financial reasons it has not been possible to make a start on the … New Buildings planned four years ago.'

25. J M Robertson and D Neave, *Francis Johnson: A Classical Statement,* 92.

26. *Ibid,* 94.

27. Gary Cox, St Chad's bursar, 2 November 2012, pers comm.

28. DULSC UND/F3/C3/A2.

29. DULSC UND/F3/C3/A4 (7)+(10).

30. DULSC UND/F3/C3/A6 (6).

31. DULSC UND/F3/C3/A6 (8).

32. DULSC notes.

33. T E Yates, *A College Remembered St John's College Durham 1909-2000* 2nd edition (Durham 2001), 17.

34. Amabel Craig (ed), *Fides Nostra Victoria – A Portrait of St John's College, Durham,* 2008, 67.

35. *Op cit,* Yates, 30.

36. *Ibid.*

37. *Ibid,* 92–3.

38. *Op cit,* Craig 65.

39. M McMurray, 'Eden House' – student dissertation.

40. Revd Prof. S L Greenslade, 'The Site of St John's College 1541-1800', *The Durham Johnian,* 2, Jan 1948, 6–10.

41. *Op cit,* Johnson.

42. *Op cit,* Yates, 65.

43. Purcell Miller Triton, 'Heritage and Condition Survey of the Castle Walls on the Durham Peninsula', unpublished report for Durham City Council.

44. *Op cit,* Craig, 66.

45. *Op cit,* Yates, 66, Plans to knock down the barn between 5 and 6 first mentioned in 1957. Site cleared 1960/1, foundation stone laid 1961.

46. Norman Emery, 'Excavations at the Church of St Mary-the-Less, Durham City', *Durham Archaeological Journal,* 18, 2009, 23–38, and Peter Ryder, *St Mary-the-Less, Durham An Archaeological Assessment,* August 1998.

47. *Op cit,* Craig 77.

48. H Tudor, *St Cuthbert's Society,* 2–14.

49. *Ibid,* 14.

50. *Ibid,* 90.

51. *Ibid,* 112–15.

52. *Ibid,* 132.

53. The Count's House lies just outside the present university land, now owned by the Chapter of Durham Cathedral.

CHAPTER 5

1. COLLEGE BIBLIOGRAPHY:

   E F Braley, *The College of the Venerable Bede.*

   Angel Lawrence, *St Hild's College, 1858-1958,* Durham, 1958.

   Donald E Webster, *Bede College – A commentary,* Durham, 1973.

   Ian Booth, *The College of St Hild and St Bede, Durham,* Durham, 1979.

   Kenneth Wilkinson, 'The Durham Diocesan Training School for Masters 1839-1886', M Ed Thesis, no date (not consulted).

2. E F Braley, *The College of the Venerable Bede.*

3. Booth says differently – site transferred 1845, works started 1845, buildings finished 1847.

4. Cathedral Archives. Architectural Drawings. DCD/N/CA 29–34.

5. Donald E Webster, *Bede College – A commentary,* Durham, 1973, 24.

6. *Ibid.* Whole of west end remodelled and extended 1928–31.

7. *Ibid,* 30.

8. *Ibid.*

9 Webster notes that the altar crucifix was designed by S E Dykes-Bower, and was intended for one of the Bede Chapel in the Cathedral Nine Altars, until its installation there was opposed by one of the cathedral canons.

10 Ian Booth, *The College of St Hild and St Bede, Durham*, Durham, 1979, Fig 26.

11 Revd Fr Jonathan Lawson, college chaplain, suggests wood is walnut and mahogany, email 28-11-2012.

CHAPTER 6
1 DULSC UND/CC1/R8 1956–7.

2 *Ibid*.

3 KINGSGATE BRIDGE BIBLIOGRAPHY:

Nikolaus Pevsner and Elizabeth Williamson, *Buildings of England: County Durham*, 1983, 2nd ed., 230–1.

Architectural Review, 135, 1964, 264–6.

Northern Architect, March 1966, 645–7.

OVE ARUP BIBLIOGRAPHY:

Arup, Ove Nyquist, Liengaard, Anja. ed. *Doodles and doggerel*. London, 1989.

Brawne, Michael, *Arup Associates: The biography of an architectural practice*. London, 1983.

Campbell, Peter; Allan, John; Ahrends, Peter; Zunz, Jack; Morreau, Patrick (1995). *Ove Arup 1895-1988*. London, 1995.

Jones, Peter (2006). *Ove Arup: Masterbuilder of the Twentieth Century*, Yale, 2006.

Ove Arup & Partners 1946-1986. London, 1986.

Churchill Archives Centre, *The Papers of Sir Ove Arup*.

DUNELM HOUSE BIBLIOGRAPHY:

Architectural Review, Oct 1963, 282.

Building, 17 Aug 1966, 403–4.

Interior Design, Nov 1966, 518–23.

The Architect's Journal, 15 June 1966, 1483–93.

The Architect's Journal, 10 May 1972, 1017–28.

Nikolaus Pevsner and Elizabeth Williamson, *Buildings of England: County Durham*, 1983, 2nd ed., 233–4.

Elain Harwood, 'Dunelm House, University of Durham', English Heritage internal report, unpublished.

Alan Powers, 'A thoughtful Brutalism', *Twentieth Century Society Magazine*, Spring, 2012.

4 Professor Douglass Wise, Head of the School of Architecture, Newcastle University pers comm., in a lecture to architecture students, *c*.1970.

5 *Architectural Review*, 135, 1964, 264–6.

6 *Northern Architect*, March 1966, 646.

7 DULSC UND/CH3/172, Notes by Nick Holmes, University of Sheffield, July 2010. Building illustrated in *The Builder* 13 October 1944, 290–3.

8 Notes by Nick Holmes, University of Sheffield, July 2010, in DUL.

9 *Architectural Review*, 139, 1966, 461 – says Dick Raine was 'architect-in-charge', but this is misleading as Powers evidently ran the job as an A-CP partner.

10 DULSC UND/CH1/A153, Dunelm House, (Feb 1961 – July 1963).

11 Documented in DUL UND/CH4/A136-138.

12 DULSC UND/CH4/A137, 10 July 1962.

13 *Ibid*, 6 December 1963.

14 *Durham University Journal 1894*.

CHAPTER 7
Most of the references in this chapter relate to building architects and dates, usually obtained through the good offices of the Estates and Buildings Department of Durham University. One exception is the published account of the early William Whitfield building, known as the West Building, which appeared in two 1952 journals – *Building*, October 1952, 372–80 and *Architects' Journal*, 24 July 1952, 104–10.

CHAPTER 8
1 Elizabeth B Boyd, *St Mary's College, University of Durham 1899-1999: A Centenary Review*, 1999, 9.

2 *Ibid*, 27.

3 *Ibid*, 28–9.

4 Elain Harwood, biographical notes on Vincent Harris, English Heritage report, unpublished.

5 *Ibid*, 29.

6 *St Mary's College Newsletter* 1946–7, 3–4.

7 *St Mary's College Newsletter* 1951–2, 1–2.

8 *St Mary's College Newsletter* 1948–9, 3.

9 *Op cit*, Boyd, 42.

10 *Ibid*, 45.

11 *Ibid*.

12 *Ibid*, 49.

13 Harris's comments on landscaping from Building Committee minutes.

14 DULSC UND/CP2/75-9.

15 Susan Martin, *Trevs: A Celebration of 40 Years of Trevelyan College, Durham*, 2006, 9.

16 *Ibid*, 12 DULSC UND/CH4/A24-26.

17 *Ibid*.

18 *Ibid*, 16.

19 *Ibid*.

20 Professor Ann Moss, pers comm.

21 *Ibid*, 18.

22 Elain Harwood, English Heritage report on Durham University, unpublished.

23 *Ibid*, 83.

24 *Ibid*, 86.

25 *Ibid*, 112–14.

26 *Ibid*, 89–90.

27 *Ibid*, 111–12.

28 *Ibid*, 94–96.

29 Notes on Southend by Mary Apperley, former resident. Personal copy, copy also in DUL: Special Collections.

30 DULSC UND/CH4/A12, 13 February 1961.

31 *Ibid*, 21 February 1962.

32 C Barclay, R Groke, H Armstrong, (eds), *Treasures of the Oriental Museum, Durham University*, 2010, 14.

33 Dr Craig Barclay pers comm.

34 Graham E Rodmell, *St Aidan's: from Home students to Society to College*, University of Durham, 1997, 2.

35 *Ibid*, 10.

[36] *Ibid*, 20.

[37] *Ibid*, 53.

[38] *Ibid*, 55.

[39] *Ibid*.

[40] DULSC UND/CH4/A4, Jan 1960. The architects were A G MacDonald, E Armstrong + F MacManus, Tripe & Wakemen, and Covell & Matthews. Elain Harwood, in a note to the author, comments, 'Alistair MacDonald must have been getting elderly, son of Ramsay MacDonald the Prime Minister, and known to me for his cinemas in the 1930s. He also extended Toynbee Hall, the settlement that Clem Attlee was much involved with. Some commercial work for Shell in the 1950s. Armstrong + MacManus are the best known of this group, as specialist housing architects. Frederick MacManus had worked for Thomas Tait, Burnet Tait & Lorne, notably at Silver End for Critalls in the late 1920s. Post-war they pretty much concentrated on public housing, for which they were highly regarded. Tripe & Wakeham are northern architects, but had a big commercial practice that continues today. Covell & Matthews were a big church practice in London, for the diocese of London, but also had a big commercial practice – Piccadilly Plaza in Manchester is perhaps their best-known work. What an odd assortment. They must have all been known to members of the university's council/committee. Spence is well-known for never turning a job down, and was already working for the then Durham University at Newcastle (Herschel Building for Physics).'

[41] *Ibid*.

[42] *Op cit*, Rodmell, 56.

[43] DULSC UND/CH2/139, 13 June 1960.

[44] *Ibid*, 23 August 1960.

[45] Elain Harwood, English Heritage report, unpublished.

[46] *Op cit*, DULSC UND/CH4/A4, Letter 13 October 1961.

[47] Chapel of Unity and Chapel of Christ the Servant or Guild Chapel.

[48] *Op cit*, Rodwell, 101.

[49] *Ibid*, 60.

[50] *Ibid*, 167.

[51] G D Rochester and G M Parton, 'The Durham Obelisk', *Durham Archaeological Journal*, 2, 1986, 107.

[52] Jill Allibone, *Anthony Salvin: Pioneer of Gothic Revival Architecture 1799-1881*, 1987, 133.

[53] *Op cit*, Rochester and Parton, 107.

[54] *Op cit*, Allibone, 134.

[55] *Ibid*.

[56] Durham University Library notes.

[57] Statutory List of Buildings of Architectural of Historic Interest – description.

[58] *Op cit*, Rochester and Parton, 105.

CHAPTER 9

[1] Nigel Watson, *From the Ashes: the story of Grey College, Durham*, (Durham 2004), 17.

[2] DULSC UND/F8/C1/E6 University Building Committee Minutes 1945–51, 11-1-1949.

[3] *Op cit*, Watson, 17.

[4] DULSC UND/CC1/R8, 3-7-56, 16-7-56. In early July of that year Allen generously wrote to Worthingtons to congratulate them on their appointment, only to write again a fortnight later, noting that he had already prepared a fully drawn scheme but received little fee. Allen was in dispute with the college's appointed engineer. The Warden was perplexed by Allen's behaviour.

[5] *Op cit*, Watson.

[6] *Ibid*.

[7] *Ibid*.

[8] *Ibid*, 18.

[9] *Ibid*.

[10] N Pevsner, *Buildings of England: County Durham*, 2nd edition, 1983, 237.

[11] *Ibid*.

[12] COLLEGE BIBLIOGRAPHY: Article by Anthony Williams & Burles, 'Collingwood College, Durham; Architects: Richard Sheppard, Robson & Partners', *Building*, vol. 227, no. 6840 (28), 1974 July 12, pp.79–86;'Architecture plus', *1974 RIBA Awards*, vol. 2, no. 6, 1974 Nov./Dec., p.104.

[13] Anthony Tuck, *Collingwood College, University of Durham: A Jubilee History 1972-1997*, 1997, 7–27.

[14] Listing description: House. Early, mid and later C19; Flemish bond brick garden front, coursed squared sandstone rear; rear wing sandstone with brick and ashlar dressings; Welsh slate roof with brick chimneys and rendered chimney at rear of wing. L-plan. Garden front two storeys, three bays, the outer bays canted. Central French window and overlight; other windows sashes with glazing bars; flat stone lintels, some with bracketed cornices, and projecting stone sills. Bracketed moulded gutter. Low-pitched hipped roof has later central dormers. Garden wall attached to right return; sandstone outer leaf, brick inner, with flat stone coping; segmental-headed doorway to lane. From 1850 to 1852 this was the home of Revd John Bacchus Dykes, hymn writer; Precentor of Durham Cathedral and vicar of St Oswald's church, Durham. Included for historic interest.

[15] BBC Music website.

[16] *Building*, 9 June 2000, 37.

[17] HOWLANDS FARM COLLEGE DUL REFERENCES. UND/F2/E1 July 1997: 'Howlands Trust Project 1993-1997. A1: List of what was done with the project files at its winding up in July 1997. Compiled by Margaret Creighton, secretary to the Principal Designate.' DULSC UND/F2/E2 July 1997: 'List with commentary by Miss Deborah Lavin, Principal Designate, of the topical files of the project deposited in the University Library's Archives & Special Collections, Compiled July 1997 [i.e. list of files in section (of the deposit)].' DULSC UND/CH2/B24 February – August 2003: Dunelm Student Villages Colleges Accommodation Project plans for the Howland Farm and Parsons Field sites, by Gotch Saunders & Surridge, architects.

CHAPTER 10

[1] John Haywood, Breaking *the Mould: The Surprising Story of Stockton – The First Ten Years of the University of Durham's Stockton Campus*, 2003, 12–14.

[2] *Ibid*, 15.

APPENDIX: INDEX

B

Principal locations are entered in **bold.** Illustrations are entered in *italics*. Entries, unless otherwise specified, are in Durham or its environs.

Cromwell, Oliver 35
Crossgate *17*, 73
Crozier, Mr 87
Cruddas House 72, 75
Cullen, Gordon 10, 142
Cusdin, Burden & Howitt 104
Cuthbert, St 8, 26, 27

DARBYSHIRE ARCHITECTS 73
Dawson Building *18–19*, 19, 104, 136
Dean and Chapter 16, 19, 41, 83, 108 *see also* Durham Cathedral
Dennis Lister & Associates 147
Development Plan 24, 111
Dewjoc 104, 106
Diocesan Training Institution 83
doorcases 99, *99*
Douai 150
Dower, Robin 127
Duff, Sir James 88, 125
Dun Cow Lane 12, 40, 53, 62, 66
Dunbar, Battle of 35
Dunelm House **92–4**; designers of 90; Kingsgate Bridge and 15, 89, *89*; Napper's master plan 23; photographs *93*, *94*; river and 11–12
Dunn & Hansom 150
Durham Castle **27–38**; appropriated 17; Framwellgate Bridge view 12; Normans 8; Pace quoted 49; view from Crossgate *17*
Durham Cathedral *see also* Dean and Chapter architects 17, 48; college panoramas 119; Cosin's work 35, 46; Framwellgate Bridge view 12; Little High Wood backdrop 106; Nine Altars chapel 12, 66, 125; Normans 8; revelatory view 11; view from west *9*
Durham County Advertiser 98
Durham Miners' Gala 101
Durham Student Theatre 53
Dutton, John 43
Dykes, Revd John Bacchus 138

EASTON, ROBERTSON, CUSDIN, PRESTON & SMITH 104
Eastwick-Field, John 114, 115, 117

Ebsworth Building 147, *147*
Eden, Sir John 73; Eden family 72, 75; Eden House 73
Edwards, John 43
EGG building 104
Eggleston Hall, 123
Elgey, Charles 53
Elsey, Bob 48
Eltham Palace, London 84
Elvet 23, 89, 131 *see also* New Elvet; Old Elvet
Elvet Bridge 23, 98; Elvet Garth 111; Elvet Hill 24, 114, 118, 119, **122–3**, 124; Elvet Riverside 23, 95–6, *96*; Elvethall 97
Engineering Science Department 104
English College, Douai 150
English Department 100
English Landscape movement 10
Erskine, Ralph 128
Estates and Buildings Department 111, 135
Etsuko Hall 113
Euston Station, London 58
Exchequer 43, *43*, **44–5**, *44*, *45*, 48
Expedition Engineering 148

FABER, OSCAR 43
Fadden, Mary 118
Faulkner Brown, Hendy, Watkinson & Stonor, 103, 104, 127
Fellows' Garden 37, 38, *39*
Festival of Britain 103, 111
Fiennes, Celia 81
First World War 69
Fives Court 43
Fleshergate 10
Fletcher Joseph, architects 147
Fogg-Elliott family 118, 123
Fountains Field 130; Fountains Hall *132*
Fowler, Charles Hodgson 58
Framwellgate 83, 84; Framwellgate Bridge 12, *13*, 81
Fraunhofer Refractor equatorial telescopes 129
Frost, Terry 105
Fulling Mill 81, *81*

GARDEN STAIR BUILDING 29
Geography Department 103, 104
Gibside 75
Gilesgate 21, 87
Gilly, Revd WS 122
Glasgow School of Art 49
Grants Committee 110, 114, 119, 126, 133, 134
Grey, Charles, 2nd Earl 130
Grey College 23, 24, 60, 88, 119, **130–3**
GSS Architecture 43, 106, 128, 141, 147
Gulbenkian Foundation 123
Gulbenkian Museum of Oriental Art 119, 123

HACKETT, BRIAN 115, 126, 135
Hallgarth House 96–7; Hallgarth Street 89, 96
Halliday Meecham Architects 147
Hansom, Joseph 150
Hardwick, Philip 58
Harris, Vincent 59, 92, *93*, **108–13**
Harrogate Design Group 43
Harrying of the North 27
Harwood, Elain 49, 126
Hatfield College (formerly Hatfield Hall) **54–60**; Bailey Court and 39; Birley Room 6; chapel arches *142*; Church Street sites 96; David Roberts rebuilds 53; design features 50; founded 17; gardens below 81; origins 52; riverbank terrace *143*; staircase *71*
Haughton House 72, 73
Hawkins Heath Partnership 106
Heath, John (IV) 55
Henrietta Maria, Queen 45
Henry VIII, King, of England 16
Herschel Building 125
Hicks, HL 62
Hicks, WS 87
Hild College 18, *18* see also College of St Hild and St Bede; St Hild's College
Himalayan Collection 137
HLB Architects 73
Holgate House 132-3

Holliday, Professor Fred 146
Holliday Building *146–7*, 147
Hollingside 24, 130–2, *131*, 136–7, **138**, *139*
Hooton Pagnall 62
Howarth Litchfield Partnership 43, 128, 132
Howison, John 87
Howlands Farm 24, 136, 139, *140*
Hussey, Revd TJ 129
Hyland, Sheila 136

ICE HOUSE 79
Infinity Bridge 148, *148*
Ingram, Edward 62
Institute for Middle East and Islamic Studies 128, *128*
Institute of Hazard and Risk Research 22, 103, *103*
Iron Age 8, 107

JAMES VI, KING OF SCOTLAND 35
James Barber House 96
Jenkinson, Dr John Banks 16
Jesus Mill 81
Jevons House 58, 59, 60
John Snow College 147
Johnson, Francis 60, **62–6**, 68, 78
Jones, Dennis 38, 117, 132
Jones, WT 59
Joseph Potts & Sons 87
Josephine Butler College 24, 136, 137, **139–41**
Junior Common Rooms: Collingwood 134; Grey 133; St Cuthbert's

KEMPE, STAINED GLASS 38
Kepier Hospital 55, 57
King's College (Newcastle) 19, 23
Kingsgate Bridge **90–3**; adjacent buildings 96; Bow Lane and *144–5*; Dunelm House and 15, 89, *89*, 94; from New Elvet *11*; Napper's master plan 23; planning consent 93; river and 12, *12*

LAFCADIO HEARN CENTRE 113, *113*
Laud, Archbishop 45

157

APPENDIX: ACKNOWLEDGEMENTS

C

Writing a book like this one depends so much upon the collaboration of other people. You need them to guide you through archives, to explain the workings of the university, and to open doors and invite you in. In a wider sense you need their encouragement too, and I've been blessed with helpful and welcoming contacts throughout.

My special thanks must first go to Prof Chris Higgins, the Vice-Chancellor, for asking me to write the book, and having the faith that I would deliver it. Thanks also to Jon Purcell, the University Librarian, my regular contact and the following university staff: Dr Sheila Hingley, Dr Michael Stansfield, Caroline Craggs and all staff in Special Collections, Palace Green Library. Harvey Dowdy, Jane Taylor, Emma Chapman, Matthew Wright, Michael Forster and Philippa Greenwood of the Estates and Buildings Office, Michele Allan (Cartographic Unit, Department of Geography). Also Paulina Lubacz, Deborah Monk, Dr Henry Dyson, Dr Ian Doyle, Prof Ann Moss, Alison Holmes, Rebecca Grundy and Rebecca Turnbull.

Thanks to Dr Craig Barclay, Rachel Grocke (Oriental Museum), Jackie Carr (Assembly Rooms), Stephen Ansdell (Botanic Garden) and David Fionda (Queens Campus), and at the following colleges – Richard Brickstock (University), Prof. Tim Burt, Katie Petherick, Bill Moyes (Hatfield), Revd Canon Dr Joseph Cassidy, Gary Cox, Jane Manley, Ian Henderson, (St Chad's), Revd Prof. David Wilkinson, Dr Campbell Grant, Liz Forbes (St John's), Chris Finnemore (St Cuthbert's), Revd Fr Jonathan Lawson, Joanne Moorhouse, Jane Young (St Hild and St Bede), Prof. Simon Hackett, Martin Clemmett, Richard Hird, Carole Laverick (St Mary's), Karen Blundell (Grey), Prof. Joe Elliott (Collingwood), Prof. David Harper, Paula Dawson (Van Mildert), Prof. Martyn Evans (Trevelyan), Prof. Susan Frenk (St Aidan's) and Adrian Simpson (Josephine Butler). Thanks also to Gabriel Sewell and Catherine Turner (Durham Cathedral Library).

A number of non-university friends were always on hand to answer my questions. My thanks to Jenifer White, Elain Harwood, Dennis and Jo Jones, Dr Douglas Pocock, John Jennings, Sandra Robertson, David Sparke, Catherine Dewar, Robin Dower, Roger Norris, Dr Myra Tolan-Smith, Tony Smith, Keith Blundell, Nick Owen, Fiona Green, David Butler and Richard Hewlings. Also Liz Bregazzi and Gill Parkes (DCRO).

Thanks also to a number of the individuals noted above who assisted in the sourcing of images. A full list of illustration acknowledgements and copyright details is given at the end of the book. At Third Millennium I'm grateful for regular advice and support from Joel Burden, Christopher Fagg and Matt Wilson. Particular thanks to John Donoghue for his brilliant photographs that capture the essence of this book. Also thanks to Royston Thomas for the use of his earlier photographs.

Finally I must thank my three children, David, Mary and William, whose encouragement throughout and critical judgements in the reading of the final draft, have made this a much better book than it was.